GROWING
THROUGH
DISASTER

CLAYTON L. **SMITH**   MATT **SCHOENFELD**

GROWING
THROUGH
DISASTER

Tools for
Financial and Trauma Recovery
in Your Faith Community

 Abingdon Press

Nashville

GROWING THROUGH DISASTER:
Tools for Financial and Trauma Recovery in Your Faith Community

Library of Congress Cataloging-in-Publication Data has been requested.

ISBN 978-1-5018-9091-8

19 20 21 22 23 24 25 26 27 28—10 9 8 7 6 5 4 3 2 1
MANUFACTURED IN THE UNITED STATES OF AMERICA

To Mary Josephine Reed,
whose legacy of mercy, kindness, and generosity
to all those in need continues to inspire us
to reach out with the hope of Jesus Christ

CONTENTS

Acknowledgments   ix

Preface   xi

Introduction: The Path to Healing   xv

Part I: Relief, Recovery, and Restoration—Three Essentials
    Chapter 1: Relief—How the Church Can Help   5
    Chapter 2: Recovery—Five Steps for Trauma Healing   17
    Chapter 3: Restoration—Reigniting Hope   29

Part II: Financial Foundations and Recovery
    Chapter 4: Assessment—Taking Your Financial Pulse   43
    Chapter 5: Spending Plan—Money Management Strategies   55
    Chapter 6: Planning—Your Financial Recovery Plan   71

Part III: Six Small Group Studies
    Chapter 7: Victim and Volunteer—Caring Matters   87
    Chapter 8: Five Tasks for Trauma Healing   95
    Chapter 9: Reigniting Hope through Love   101
    Chapter 10: Recovering Your Financial Life   107
    Chapter 11: Building Your Money Management Plan   115
    Chapter 12: Planning for Your Financial Future   123

Appendix
    A. Additional Recovery Tools   133
    B. Disaster Recovery Group Guidelines   141
    C. Community Promotion   145
    D. Volunteer Training Resources   147

Contents

E. Next Steps to Volunteer   149
F. Sample Volunteer Covenant   151
G. Closing Healing Ceremony and Celebration for
    Small Group Members   153

Notes   155

ACKNOWLEDGMENTS

I am most grateful for the witness of disaster victims and survivors who have demonstrated great faith and resilience. More specifically, I was first compelled to write this book during a Hurricane Katrina recovery project. Over a three-year period our church teams were helping homeowners rebuild their damaged homes. I witnessed victims who had lost so much grow in faith and become volunteers to others in need. God was at work to bring something good out of something horrific. Their witness of faith was real and life changing! Thank you to those unnamed and countless people and communities of faith who turn tragedy into triumph!

Secondly, I must thank the four local churches where I served for their amazing response during times of disasters. Thank you, Schweitzer, Manchester, Centenary, and Resurrection United Methodist Churches. It is the faith community that will continue to make a difference around the world through mission outreach. Abingdon Press is to be commended for publishing this vital tool to help disaster volunteers and victims! Disasters of all kinds demand the best resources possible.

Finally, I have been blessed by my staff partners, Nancy Brown and Linda Roser, who collaborated and worked with me in the technical writing process. I must also thank Matt for his outstanding partnership in this writing project to help people with financial and trauma recovery tools. Together, Matt and I offer our gifts, tools, and experience to bring help and hope to a world in need.

—Clayton Smith

I would like to first thank Clayton for inviting me to join him on this journey of writing *Growing through Disaster* together. After a decade hiatus in producing a book, it has been a pleasure working with you. Thanks for encouraging me to pick up the pen again! I greatly appreciate your deep desire to help others turn tragedy to triumph, just as you did in your life. Additionally, I would like to thank Connie Stella and her team at Abingdon Press for your vision and insight for how this book can help others, and for your assistance in the many steps needed to bring a resource like this together. Finally, to my business partners and to my family, thank you for giving me the latitude to work on this project amidst all the regular chaos of life, work, and raising teenagers.

—Matt Schoenfeld

PREFACE

Clayton's Story

It really is a double disater if you try to go it alone.

While in seminary, I was interviewing for a clinical hospital chaplain's internship, and the chaplain said, "Clayton, everything in your life has gone well. You have been blessed." Then he asked me, "Clayton, what are you going to do when something bad happens to you?"

I will never forget his question; sometimes it has haunted me. But it saved me when I really needed it. When disaster struck, it was not a natural disaster. It was a very personal disaster. In 1984 my wife of thirteen years died after a sudden and short thirty-hour illness. In spite of the crisis medical attention she received in two hospitals, she could not be saved. What do we do after such a devastating loss? What was I going to do?

With no warning, I became a single-parent pastor with two small children. I was facing the loss of the love of my life and caring for my small children, while still providing leadership and care to my church flock. I wondered if I would be able to survive when I felt like the worst thing in the world had happened to me, and I struggled.

That chaplain's challenging question came back to me. I told myself that I was not going to let this personal loss destroy me, my family, or my ministry. And I did survive, thanks to the grace of God and the support of my local church. Family and friends would not let me go it alone. From this loss, I wanted to learn to be a better father, friend, and pastor. I began *growing through my grief and personal disaster*.

My loss was also a loss for our church. If I had been unable to go on, the church and its ministries would have suffered. But, amazingly, the church survived and even thrived. People in the church and community felt a call to action to support me and my young family. They showed resilience and determination to keep me and the church going. Six years later, our denomination recognized the church with a national award for church growth (1990 Circuit Rider Publishing House Award–Schweitzer UMC, Springfield, Missouri). Because I chose not to go it alone, and our church offered such a supportive faith community, I can look back and say, we grew through disaster together.

In the aftermath of my wife's death, I started a Crisis Support Group for people dealing with trauma and loss. People in the community were in need, just as I was, and providing help for others was healing for me. In the thirty-five years since that time, I have given leadership to support groups in a number of other faith communities and have led relief and work teams to five disaster areas. I look back over these years and see how my hope helped my family heal. My second marriage was to a very compassionate woman, and we had two more wonderful children. I now have two grandchildren! I believe I have be twice blessed in marriage and have an amazing family.

As a first responder, I have observed many faith communities impacted by natural disaster. Each time I left one of these communities, I wished there was something more we could leave them with, a helpful tool or some way to provide further help. If you are a responder providing relief and aid, perhaps you too have felt this.

Growing through Disaster is just such a tool. First responders, relief teams, and community leaders can have this book in their back pockets, so to speak, ready to offer in the aftermath of any disaster. It will help people who are dealing with personal and spiritual trauma, grief, and financial loss. It is for individuals *and* for groups.

Support groups are particularly effective for helping people and communities after disaster or times of loss. When the time is right, faith communities can facilitate and host these groups. Together with others from the community, people will experience personal and spiritual healing. They'll take important steps toward long-term financial recovery. Individuals and families will begin to find wholeness, and all will see hope and a way to go on, together. The book includes six small group sessions and a plan for a special healing service to conclude the group sessions.

I've come to realize over the years how many lessons I learned from my own disaster recovery. That journey and the experiences I've had in thirty-five years as a pastor laid the foundation for this book. Now I hope to help you with the personal disaster you are facing.

If you are dealing with a disaster in your personal life or community, we wrote this book for you. It may be difficult to imagine, but you will be able to help yourself. And then you will begin to help others—people in your family and faith community. You may feel weak, but you will grow stronger.

Matt's Story

It is revealing how God often uses events and circumstances to change our course and bring about his purposes. My entire life's work and ministry came about due to a financial disaster. I got fired. Truly, it was the best thing that ever happened to me! I won't bore you with the gory details of my tumultuous rise and fall, but suffice it to say I had gone down the wrong path and was in a job that was not a good fit for a variety of reasons. Like an earthquake, I never saw it coming, and my world was shaken. At age thirty-six, I was out on my ear with no career, no income, and two small children and my wife to feed and support.

Only God can take a mess like that, and in a few short months, turn it into a financial stewardship ministry that had me impacting thousands and thousands of people all across the United States and select places around the globe. It is a poignant reminder of how God uses the broken to bring about his plan. Plus, I never would have met Clayton had I not gotten my pink slip! Clayton and I are convinced from our own ordeals, and from ministering to thousands, that when we turn to God in our time of distress—our time of trauma—Christ will meet us and provide exceedingly more than we could ever hope or imagine.

By no means are we saying this will be easy or pleasant. However, when you get to the recovery side and look back (and we are both praying for every person who reads this book that God will carry you there!), you will see the hand of God moving and the love of God providing for you.

For nearly thirty years, (with the exception of the above-mentioned ten-month hardship detour), my entire career has been devoted to helping people learn to manage money according to bedrock biblical financial principles. After three decades of serving as a financial coach and advisor, I have seen my fair share of financial disaster and trauma situations. Whether it was a young widow who was left with little income and insufficient life insurance proceeds, a crushing divorce situation that decimated the now-single mom financially, or a well-meaning husband who blew the retirement fund making terrible, speculative investment decisions, I have helped thousands of people take their financial disaster situation and turn it into a testimony of God's goodness and faithfulness.

In *Growing through Disaster*, my hope is that Clayton and I can provide real-world, useful, simple tools and resources to help you begin to rebuild your financial and spiritual world after a natural or personal disaster. I have had the good fortune over the years to partner with a number of international compassionate ministry programs providing relief to the less fortunate. It has been one of my life's passions to help find ways to connect kingdom resources to those around the globe who need the love of Christ and the basic necessities of life to make it through to the next day. I pray that this book can in some way help you and your faith community tap into resources and the power of the Holy Spirit (truly the greatest resource working in your situation) to help you recover from your personal disaster and grow deeper in your relationship with the One who longs to meet your every need. Only together can we overcome the tremendous challenges facing us after a disaster We hope you will use this resource and find a support group to help you grow stronger and more resilient in faith, hope, and love.

INTRODUCTION: THE PATH TO HEALING

While natural disasters capture headlines and national attention short-term,
the work of recovery and rebuilding is long-term.
—Sylvia Mathews Burwell

The water just kept rising. After living for fifty years in the same house by the creek outside of Houston, Texas, and weathering countless hurricanes without a flood, Hurricane Harvey would prove to be an altogether different proposition. Jenny, being a hurricane veteran, knew Houston was in for a serious storm, so she packed an overnight bag, put the dogs in the car, and drove the one-hour stretch to her childhood home where her ailing mother, Sarah, still lived. She planned to stay the night to help her ride out the latest storm. Then disaster struck, and it struck fast and hard.

The amount of rain that fell during Hurricane Harvey truly was of biblical proportion. In just three days, more than fifty-three inches of rain fell on Jenny and her mom, and the flooding was so severe that more than 60,000 people were displaced and more than 17,000 had to be rescued. Jenny and her mom lived out that statistic. It happened so fast they had very little time to prepare. By two a.m. on Sunday morning the water was halfway up the driveway, and by four a.m. the flood entered the house. Jenny moved quickly. Sarah was in a wheelchair, so she called the city and requested help. Sensing the severity of the flooding, she shut off the power and also called to wake up the neighbors to warn them. She swiftly stowed irreplaceable family photos and personal items on closet shelves. It wasn't much, but she knew furniture could be replaced. Photos and mementos could not.

When some Good Samaritans with a boat finally arrived at noon on Sunday, there was two feet of water in the house, and just like that, her childhood home and most everything in it was destroyed. When they left, all that made it in the boat was Jenny, her mom in her wheelchair, a suitcase of clothes, three dogs, and a bag of dog food! Looking back, she said it must have looked comical. They were transported to a church that had a temporary holding area where they stayed one night. A more significant shelter was being set up at the high school. They were told that if there was someone who could come get them soon, they could stay at the school, but otherwise they would be transported to Dallas. Not ideal. Sarah was seventy-nine years old.

No one could get across the now-bursting creek to pick them up, and Jenny's car, stuck in the flooded garage, was totaled. Fortunately, her mom had a friend who took them in, because the trauma was definitely having effect on Sarah's health. After three days with friends, they were able to place Sarah in an assisted living facility in the last room available. Tragically, the trauma of the ordeal took such a toll on Sarah, who was already suffering from early-onset dementia, that she passed away only three months after the flood.

A huge blessing in disguise was that Sarah had been wise and purchased flood insurance; thus, her house and its contents were fully covered. Members from a local church helped Jenny gut the house so that it could be refurbished, but she said it was incredibly humbling for her and Sarah to see their whole lives sitting out on the curb waiting for the refuse heap. Thanks to USAA military insurance benefits that responded with the speed and precision of our armed forces, within three weeks she had a check in hand. With Sarah in assisted living, they sold the house "as is" to a rehabber. Jenny's employer, AIG Retirement and Insurance, was also incredibly generous. They made cash payments of $2,500 to $5,000 per affected employee based on the severity of their situation to help them with short-term recovery. No repayment was expected. And despite their headquarters also being flooded out for many months, AIG worked tirelessly to contact, check on, and in some cases, rescue their staff. Many of Jenny's friends without insurance were not so lucky and lost it all. FEMA was overwhelmed and could not meet the staggering demand to inspect each home. She knows people who are still trying to get a settlement two years later. Jenny's house sat high on a hill, so it did not sustain any damage. Another blessing.

However, losing her mom so soon after the tragedy was very difficult. Grief upon grief. The recovery process would be long, and Jenny says that today she and many of her friends still have some post-traumatic stress disorder symptoms whenever there is a heavy rain. However, she was greatly encouraged to see how her fellow Houstonians responded to the disaster with helping hands and generous hearts. It restored her faith in humanity. Hurricane Harvey packed a life-altering wallop for Jenny and her family. Her story of natural disaster trauma is becoming all too common.

Tsunamis in the Indian Ocean. Hurricane Katrina. Earthquakes in Haiti, China, India, and the Middle East. Mudslides in the Philippines. Tornadoes leveling towns in Kansas and Missouri. Unprecedented flooding in Nebraska. Wildfires in California.[i] These are just a few of the more prominent natural disasters that have occurred since 2003. Nearly every corner of our country has been hit. The intensity and frequency of natural disasters has been on the rise, leading to devastating grief, trauma, and loss like Jenny and Sarah experienced. How are victims to recover?

HOW THE BOOK IS ORGANIZED

Whether you have lived through a natural disaster or are dealing with a more personal disaster such as divorce, job loss, or the death of a spouse, this book is designed to be a practical and inspirational resource to help you begin your healing process. In Part I, Clayton provides Spirit-filled wisdom and recovery tools and techniques for working through grief and trauma. Having dealt with the death of his spouse, Clayton turned that tragedy into years of compassion-based grief-recovery ministry. His firsthand knowledge and experience result in very specific practices you can employ to aid your recovery from the great loss you have experienced. In Part II, Matt provides a Bible-based financial recovery path that will aid you as you work to rebuild your financial world. For nearly thirty years, Matt has helped thousands of people with his common-sense, simple approach to dealing with money that is founded on five core biblical principles. This real-world support will result in you crafting a practical financial recovery plan. Part III offers six small group sessions, three on grief recovery and three on financial recovery. This section of the book is designed to help you join with others who are experiencing similar challenges. We hope these small groups that form around the specific type of disaster you have experienced will be the catalyst for community, healing, and hope.

WHEN TO READ THE BOOK

Every disaster is different. Local leaders should partner with churches, relief agencies, and other support agencies or ministries to assess the situation and determine when to offer or adopt this book/study. Generally speaking, it will be best for people to go through the *Growing through Disaster* program anywhere from six months to eighteen months after the event. If offered too soon, there could still be too much shock to allow participants to focus properly. If too much time elapses after the disaster, then it could be hard to address recovery in a timely fashion. We pray those leading this recovery group ministry will have wisdom to offer it in God's best timing for your situation. Let the Holy Spirit lead you.

If you are reading this book and are a first responder, pastor, civic leader, or volunteer recovery small group leader, we envision *Growing through Disaster* to be a training tool to prepare and equip you with the knowledge and skill to minister to others in need. For you, the time to read this book is now, so that you are familiar with the material before you are called upon to help in the next disaster. At that time, you may lead others through the resource, or leave it behind. In either case, a firsthand understanding of the concepts will help you serve more effectively.

WHAT TYPE OF DISASTER?

We want to acknowledge that there are many types of disasters affecting communities. We often think of natural disasters; others are less common but no less impactful. While the language and focus of this book is recovery from a natural or a personal disaster, the information offered in *Growing through Disaster* is appropriate for dealing with other events such as hazardous materials spills or contamination, civil unrest, or even a nuclear incident or other types of explosions (grain elevators, mines, or chemical factories, for instance). The scale of these events, of course, would determine the viability of recovery, but the principles in this book should be appropriate to help one deal with most types of trauma.

As you begin the difficult work of rebuilding your life post-trauma, our ardent prayer is that you will sense God's presence at every step on your recovery path: healing, binding, loving, caring, and strengthening you on your journey. From our own experience of dealing with the shock of loss, we know it can be so debilitating that you feel as if you are frozen in a block of ice with no hope of a spring thaw in sight. We have been there too. The resources and spiritual counsel found in *Growing through Disaster* will be a starting point and a catalyst to lead you to complete restoration, wholeness, and deeper faith in Jesus, the One true healer of all wounded souls.

Nahum 1:7 says, "The LORD is good, a refuge in times of trouble. He cares for those who trust in him" (NIV). In light of such suffering, we turn to the Lord for refuge. God promises to care for us at all times, including times when our lives have been turned upside down. We fervently hope this resource provides real help and a sense of the care God has for you.

PART I

RELIEF, RECOVERY, AND RESTORATION—THREE ESSENTIALS

The bottom of the soul may be in repose,
even while we are in many outward troubles;
just as the bottom of the sea is calm, while the surface is strongly agitated.
—John Wesley

Each disaster is very different and presents different levels of disaster-recovery needs. This section will focus on the phases of relief, recovery, and restoration. The initial phase after disaster is generally led by first responders—the professionals who swoop in to provide rescue and immediate stabilization. These are EMTs, military, and other local, state, and national governmental leaders.

After 2017 hurricanes Harvey, Irma, and Maria, public officials reported that natural disasters are becoming a public health "new normal" expectation. The National Aeronautics and Space Administration reported that 2018 was the fourth-warmest year on record, and twenty of the warmest years on record have occurred in the last twenty-two years. According to the National Oceanic and Atmosphere Center, 2018 brought fourteen severe weather events with a devastating cost of life and an $89.4 billion price tag. The Center for Research of Epidemiology of Disaster reported that nearly 1.8 million people in the United States and 23 million around the world were impacted by disasters in 2018.

A leading question for this book is, "How can caring communities improve our response, management, and faith-based care for people and communities after disaster strikes?" It was in 2006–2007, during two recovery projects for the people in Bay Saint Louis, Mississippi, after Hurricane Katrina that I (Clayton) first felt the urgency of this question. I realized that resources were needed for relief, recovery, and restoration *beyond* people's homes and the church's buildings. Unresolved trauma takes a personal and spiritual toll for years after the physical cleanup is finished.

This book is written with both the disaster victim and volunteer in mind. When people are suffering, God's people will respond. The University of Southern California's Center for Religion and Civic Culture reported that some 506,000 volunteers from faith-based communities and organizations responded to help in the aftermath of Hurricane Katrina. Faith communities are called to be relevant, responsive, and constantly improving our training and care with people in need. Volunteers and victims need ever-more-effective resources in order to provide lasting help, and to heal. This book is an encouraging testimony to the thousands of volunteers in mission and survivors who have and will continue to make a difference.

Chapter 1 offers a variety of *spiritual practices for relief volunteers to improve their capacity and effectiveness* in disaster relief. Key relief questions that volunteers can ask are identified. Working closely with local leaders is stressed. Good communication is vital. Volunteers do not want to add to the disaster problems that are already immeasurable. A better understanding of biblically based trauma healing to bring greater resilience is described in detail. This chapter is informed by an interview of a local church pastor who served in Gulfport, Mississippi, when his church and nearly all of his members' homes were destroyed. I first met with this pastor and his spouse during Katrina. I greatly admired their pastoral care leadership. Their dynamic church was reaching their hurting community in impactful and healing ways. More than a decade later, this pastor offers inspiration and realistic insights for our consideration.

Chapter 2 identifies five essential tasks for trauma healing and recovery to take place. Recovery is hard work. It takes time and patience. Recovery can be lonely, too, because disaster isolates people. Local faith communities are vitally important for many reasons, not the least of which is the social ties they provide, which alleviate isolation and point the way toward hope. Immediately following a disaster, the church can offer worship, even if it is in the church parking lot or a rented facility. Worship, prayer, songs, and friendship bring people together. The church, when ready, can offer recovery groups to victims so that they can better cope and become more resilient. This chapter also offers nearly twenty recovery tools and spiritual practices.

Chapter 3 addresses the long-term phases of disaster restoration and rebuilding. In this chapter, personal and spiritual resources are identified. Biblically based teachings on hope and the characteristics of God's love are essential. This chapter also explores the symbol of the cross of Christ as a reflection of God's love and as a symbol of healing hope. The cross says to us that in times of disaster, God is with us in our suffering.

The content in the first six chapters of the book provide preparation and the backdrop for the corresponding six chapters that offer studies for a six-week small group recovery program. An appendix is also provided with additional resources to aid the recovery process.

Chapter 1

RELIEF—HOW THE CHURCH CAN HELP

How you respond to the issue... is the issue.[1]
—Frankie Perez

But those who hope in the LORD will renew their strength,
They will fly up on wings like eagles;
They will run and not be tired;
They will walk and not be weary.
—Isaiah 40:31

In October 1998, Hurricane Mitch hit Central America. Over eleven thousand lives were lost. Seven thousand of those souls were from Honduras. On March 10, 1999, I (Clayton) arrived in Honduras as a volunteer missionary. Our observation team had members from seven states representing the South Central Jurisdiction of The United Methodist Church. We were there to offer hope and future help as each state would later send supplies and mission teams to assist in the recovery. The rescue work had been completed by the first responders, and the relief phase was starting in the urban and rural areas.

This major disaster had a dramatic impact on me. I still have vivid memories of the destruction and loss of life. Over the previous ten years, I had completed other mission projects in Panama, Costa Rica, and Central Mexico. My affection for the beautiful people from Central America had grown over the years. I was heartbroken to observe firsthand human suffering and tragic loss in the urban and rural areas of Honduras. We traveled slowly around the country, trying to offer hope and help where we could. We found the people of Honduras paralyzed with trauma. Our team kept asking those who met with us these simple but awkward questions:

How are you feeling?

What have you lost?

How can we best help?

For most of the Honduran church leaders and disaster victims, these questions were initially unanswerable. These people were traumatized. They were in a state of shock and disbelief. They were in a state of grief and mourning. We offered our words of care, concern, hugs, and prayers. Our team soon began to ask ourselves:

How can we best offer short-term relief based on their needs?

How can we partner with them in a way that our help meets their timetable?

How can we be careful not to do any harm or unknowingly undermine their community and church leaders?

What are their relief needs that we have the ability and resources to provide in the relief, recovery, and restoration long-term timetable?

Our team took the time each day to pray, worship, and reflect on their suffering and need. I returned home from that trip with many significant pastoral and spiritual questions. I realized that the first goal of helping others with disaster relief was *don't make it worse than it already is*. I had observed in the past how good intentions can compound problems.

PROVIDE SUPPORT FOR COMMUNITY PASTORS AND LEADERS

Leadership is the key. In times of disaster, local pastors and community leaders urgently need the support of volunteer groups to address overwhelming needs. When the faith community leaders have become disaster victims themselves, it is vitally important that they and their families also receive initial and ongoing support. Pastors, like all of us, have to care for themselves and their own families first to be effective serving others. Then local pastors and other community leaders can better identify the most immediate needs in their community. They know the contextual needs and cultural understanding of their people. They are also the most trusted. I have met local pastors and leaders who are the most courageous survivors I have ever met.

I recently visited with Pastor Rod Dickson Richel who served the Mississippi United Methodist Church in Gulfport, Mississippi, at the time of Hurricane Katrina. This church and community were totally devastated. I worked with Pastor Rod and his church members in 2006 and 2007 during relief efforts. I was impressed with his leadership and approach to community recovery. Our mission team was invited to worship and share a potluck meal with his congregation. Their church had chosen to temporarily relocate rather than immediately rebuild. They decided they should first focus on helping members of their church and community rebuild. Rod's wife, Dorothy, was a clinical counselor at the local hospital. Dorothy is also a trained and ordained pastor. Together, they really loved all people in need and went the second mile to make a difference. (I will give a detailed report of what I learned from my recent interview with Pastor Rod in chapter 7.)

One local church member and volunteer described to me the vital role of local community pastors who courageously cared for others after Hurricane Katrina. These pastors demonstrated and delivered spiritual and mental health care for everyone they met each day. They brought words of encouragement and grace. Their presence gave relief to comfort the pain and shock. They coordinated housing, food, transportation, and many other needs.

People reported that coming together to worship was the most important ministry the local church could offer because people needed God and each other. Disasters quickly isolate people. The church family gatherings encouraged faith, which also helped people overcome their fear. While some fled and evacuated the disaster area because they could not cope with the tragedy, most pastors stayed and put their peoples' needs first. Hugs, prayers, and handshakes led to greater conversation and connection. Pastoral skills and prayers for hope make a difference. Tender love and care would bond and strengthen people of the church and community together. Pastors make a difference. Volunteer teams will always be more effective if they first ask the pastors and community leaders to prioritize the most critical needs.

It is all about supporting local leaders who are daily helping to encourage disaster victims. Local leaders can make the impossible possible. Eleanor Roosevelt once said, "You can gain strength, courage and confidence by every experience in which you really stop to look fear in the face. You are able to say to yourself, 'I have lived through this horror. I can take the next thing that comes along. You must do the thing you think you cannot do.'"[2] This quote reminds us that we need to first listen and learn from the courageous local leaders. We also must cooperate with the coordinating mission agencies like the United Methodist Committee on Relief (UMCOR), Federal Emergency Management Agency (FEMA), or others. Then volunteers in mission can provide the most appropriate help and effective relief. Communication and cooperation are essential in supporting local leaders.

Bob Deits, in his book *Life after Loss*, says, "Major loss and grief that follows remain among the most misunderstood of all human experiences."[3] The best intentions may bring unintended harm because it is too easy for mission relief teams to assume that victims may think like you think or feel like you feel. Begin by getting to know those you want to help. Before arriving to the project site, research the context and culture of that community. Knowing the context and culture of the community you are serving is critical to being able to honor those you are serving. The best way to understand the community you are serving happens when you first listen, hear their concerns, and stand alongside the community leaders and relief agencies.

RECOGNIZE THE VITAL ROLE OF FAITH COMMUNITIES

There are obviously many types of disasters, from very small- to large-scale. All disasters need immediate relief and then support for the long-term recovery. Most relief teams are from faith-based communities. I have heard it said that faith-based teams are the first to arrive and the last to leave after a natural disaster. In any case, volunteers in mission really bring a great amount of hope and help as a witness of faith and Christ's love.

Many coastal states with a history of natural disasters have developed long-range relief and recovery facilities and ministries. For example, I visited with Texas church leaders to learn that they have developed a significant Disaster Recovery Plan with three area Resource Depots to aid those in need. Scott Moore remembers exactly what was going through his mind when Hurricane Harvey visited Houston, Texas. "When I saw that Harvey was going to stall over Texas and dump fifty-plus inches of rain, I knew this hurricane was going to be one of the worst flooding events Texas has ever seen," said the Texas Conference United Methodist response coordinator. Unfortunately, Moore was right.

Harvey killed over one hundred people, FEMA reported 1.2 million people asking for aid, and the National Hurricane Center called this the worst flooding disaster in US history, with an estimated damage of $125 billion. "You don't see damage until you begin to open people's doors," said Texas Conference bishop Scott Jones. "Then your heart breaks."

For decades I have seen how United Methodists in Missouri have reached out in mission to our world in need. In Puerto Rico, I saw firsthand the devastation of Hurricane Maria. These people were in desperate need of help. The Missouri area bishop, Bob Farr, traveled to Puerto Rico to survey the need for recovery aid of nearly one hundred Methodist churches. In the coming year, according to Lucas Endicott, the Missouri Conference volunteers in ministry coordinator, forty-three other teams from all over Missouri will follow. Both the victims and the volunteers will be blessed to work together.

A shining example of the church's vital role is the United Methodist Committee on Relief (UMCOR). This denominational arm extends relief to people around the world. The UMCOR staff is devoted to serving the most vulnerable communities following disaster. Thousands of volunteers receive necessary training and support each year before being sent to the mission field. The United Methodist Volunteers in Mission Network offers guidance, organization, and training through the conference disaster coordinator. Other denominations offer tremendous organization and help too.

Communities of faith hit by disaster are sometimes able to open their doors for shelter immediately. They may be able to provide help for disaster victims needing to relocate. In many cases, local church or community buildings provide meals, information, and a place of shelter to meet and connect. People of all socioeconomic levels need the welcoming reassurance of social connection. Victims come seeking care, comfort, and compassion.

The faith community can also provide needed access for worship and prayer services when facilities are available. Worship centers are also needed to provide a place for funeral and memorial services. The reading of sacred scriptures, healing prayers, and connecting to a faith community are essential for short-term and long-term healing and hope.

UNDERSTAND TRAUMA

We all need a better understanding of the dynamics and impact of trauma in our hurting world today. My first professional experience in clinical treatment for trauma was serving as a correctional caseworker at the Missouri Training School for Delinquent Boys. I was right out of college, and I had not yet started seminary. I began to realize that these youth had experienced varying degrees of trauma and developmental behavior crises. It was always important to ask, "What happened to you?" It did not help to ask, "What's wrong with you?" Developing an individual treatment plan for each youth in this clinical setting was the first step. We could diagnose the cause of the behavioral problem once the trauma was understood. Getting the youth to talk about their traumatic experience was the first step of knowing how to help. I learned to respect the power of trauma.

> In helping the victims of disasters, it is most helpful to ask and understand the story of their unique trauma.

In helping the victims of disasters, it is most helpful to ask and understand the story of their unique trauma. Telling their story gives them an opportunity to express their feelings. Expressing and experiencing deep feelings often brings relief and healing. However, for some victims, medical and mental health professionals may be needed. Healing may require a medical diagnosis in the event of physical problems, depression, grief, chronic pain, sleep problems, or irritability.

Trauma can occur when an event—in this case, some sort of disaster—causes pain or threat to the person's well-being. The traumatic event may negatively impact a person's coping skills and communication ability. Most often this is a short-term situation when coping skills are blocked because of shock and feelings of numbness. Trauma can also be understood as toxic stress. People who experience trauma have a greater risk for health issues, substance abuse, developmental issues, adoption of high-risk behaviors, and a variety of social problems.

Professional trauma care workers advise us that trauma can serve as a lens through which the individual now sees the world. It can change their perspective. While trauma healing can happen with the personal or spiritual support of family and the faith community, it may be necessary for those with chronic issues to also seek help from medical and mental health experts.[4] I have found it important to encourage those in need of extra care to first go to their primary doctor who already knows them. Their doctor can make a referral. Beware that some trauma victims will not follow through with the referral and get specialized help. Extra encouragement and follow-up may be needed to motivate victims to get care.

DISASTER-INFORMED TRAUMA

Trauma from natural disasters is one of the acute causes of ongoing suffering from an overwhelming experience. Earthquakes, hurricanes, tornadoes, fires, floods, landslides, volcanic eruptions, and tsunamis are all types of natural events that impact people everywhere around the world.

Natural disasters often come with little or no warning, and they may traumatize large numbers of people. People lose loved ones, homes, businesses, churches, and their livelihood. Helplessness, distress, and long-term suffering result. Trauma and grief reactions to loss are unique to each person and community context.

> Children and youth are especially vulnerable to trauma. For a national network of caregivers, see Adverse Childhood Experiences Connection (ACESC) at www.acesconnection.com.

Survivors need a safe place to reconnect. After victims have received relief and first aid, the shock may give way to other emotions like anxiety, anger, depression, guilt, and feelings of hopelessness. Victims may feel they are wounded by trauma and grief. They may feel betrayed, all alone, and helpless, especially as questions about God arise. When we are victims of trauma we often ask, *"Why?"* Spiritual comfort and assurance is essential for recovery.

In the aftermath of disaster, people sometimes ignore or do not even recognize the trauma wounds they or others have suffered. Trauma wounds that go without attention and care may result in long-term behavioral disorders and spiritual bankruptcy. In seminary we are taught the importance of timely pastoral intervention and care. As a pastor, I learned to minister to others with a sense of urgency to offer healing and hope.

TRAINING FOR TRAUMA-INFORMED CARE

Trauma puts a high demand on medical and mental health professionals, pastors, counselors, and caregivers. We are living with the constant threat of economic uncertainty, political conflict, violence, terrorism, natural disasters, and war. All this and many other personal trauma events continue to take a toll on people of all ages. Churches, hospitals, schools, and other institutions are seeing the training needs for trauma healing. Treatment for those with post-traumatic stress syndrome disorder is an urgent and growing need.

I was trained in crisis intervention when I served at the Suicide Prevention Center at Southern Methodist University. Over the years of pastoral ministry, I have updated and adapted what I learned. This model has been invaluable to me.

In times of crisis it is helpful to have an approach to fit to the unique needs of others. Simply put, here are proven basic pastoral care intervention steps:

Step 1—Make contact. Be there as soon as possible and listen.

Step 2—When possible, help the survivors focus and tell their situation.

Step 3—Help them find practical ways to cope and care for themselves.

Step 4—Offer hope and pray with them for God's assurance of love.

Step 5—Refer them to a faith-based support group.

Step 6—Guide them to a pathway of recovery, which may include professional referrals.

Training programs are badly needed for faith-based caregivers and volunteers. Many churches offer trauma healing training to mission teams before they serve at a disaster location. But training is needed to equip additional people for future circumstances, and to help churches meet the needs in their own communities when they arise. An American Red Cross poll taken almost a month after the September 11, 2001, terrorist attacks indicated that close to 60 percent of those polled were likely or very likely to seek help from a spiritual counselor, as opposed to only 40 percent who were likely or very likely to seek help from a mental health professional.[5] This statistical survey tells us that most people want and need spiritual help.

The American Psychological Association urges trauma relief caregivers to help victims realize they are not alone. A sense of spiritual community can be vital for recovery. Many people want and need to find peace with God. The faith community can offer worship services, support groups, pastoral counseling, and many other forms of care. The faith community can also facilitate victims helping each other, developing even stronger community bonds.

BUILDING RESILIENT FAITH COMMUNITIES

On May 22, 2013, the second anniversary of the Joplin F5 tornado, former secretary of Homeland Security Janet Napolitano came to Joplin, Missouri, to present its citizens the first ever Rick Rescorla National Award for Resilience. Guest speaker at the event was long-time Joplin resident and civic volunteer Jane Cage said:

> I've seen men and women bend but not break beneath the load of responsibilities heaped upon them by May 22. I've seen tired faces around the meeting table as we pushed and planned. I've also seen a community that dared to dream by writing their vision on sticky notes in a crowded gymnasium. I've seen us recognize our potential and grow bold to reach for what we could become. I've been heartened time after time when we have put our individual organizational needs aside to work for the common good.[6]

Resilience is the ability to withstand or recover quickly from difficult conditions. For example, some coastal communities have developed resilience from multiple hurricane disasters. People who have recovered from one disaster may be able to demonstrate greater resilience when there is the next disaster. However, if there are people who have unhealed trauma wounds, a second disaster may compound their problems.

The Blessing by Gary Smalley and John Trent offers good advice for those initial encounters with people after a disaster. We can offer a meaningful touch or gesture when we first meet those in need. Sharing the right spoken words of care and concern is vital. Expressing acceptance and genuine value of the person and their pain is a priority. And finally, your sincere commitment to help motivates and leads the trauma victim to act. Even small things bring great comfort.[7]

After a disaster, symptoms of previous unhealed traumatic events and destructive behaviors may surface. While it is true that disasters may bring out the best in people; it is also true that for some it brings out the worst behavior. Our communities of faith can make greater and lasting impact when they are trained and prepared to offer trauma healing ministries. Small group ministry, especially, that offers trauma healing can really change lives with the assurance of faith and hope. As churches grow in their awareness and skill of trauma healing ministry they will multiply impact and mission, and will contribute to the long-term resilience of their communities.

NEEDED RESOURCES

This book encourages pastors and volunteer leaders to provide trauma healing training classes and resources for disaster recovery. While serving in the Katrina disaster recovery, I observed that pastors who collaborated with each other before, during, and after the crisis were more effective in trauma healing. Faith leaders can help by partnering with other professionals who serve those who are facing trauma-related issues and challenges. Together, the medical, mental health, and education leaders can look to the church to organize community-wide programs that bring courageous and hope-filled living in uncertain times. Be prepared!

Symptoms of trauma wounds:

Intense personal feelings

Unpredictable feelings

Flashbacks that haunt

Vivid memories

Confusion

Difficulty with decisions

Sleeping and eating disorders

Fear and loss of faith and trust

Physical symptoms such as anxiety, headaches, nausea, pain, and confusion

Trauma victims need a safe place for mourning, spiritual healing, and trauma recovery. They need support for their family, friends, and neighbors. While there may be others who may also need professional help to regain control of their personal lives, the road to recovery can begin in the faith community. Daniel Aldrich, PhD, author of the book *Building Resilience*, makes an important observation from his research that having strong social connections really makes a significant difference in disaster and trauma healing.[9] Faith-based communities offer vital social connections and events that build lifelong relationships.

Throughout history, priests, pastors, and chaplains have been helpers for others in time of disaster. Today, lay ministers of every faith can also be called and trained to help in times of need and crisis. There is an opportunity in every challenge for the faith community to make a difference and a greater impact. Pastors and faith-based leaders are often unsung community caregivers, heroes, and heroines! And yet, God blesses those who serve others in times of crises.

The significant impact of crisis support groups cannot be overstated. I facilitated Growing through Grief groups for twenty years during my ministry in three different faith communities. In each community, I saw healing happen, lives changed, and the church's impact on the community grow. In the last church I served, we offered many small groups each week through the discipleship and pastoral care ministries. For twelve years I co-facilitated a men's cancer support group. I have often observed that people who have gone through a traumatic event can become outstanding small group facilitators when given training and support. These support groups make the work of the church relevant to people's urgent needs. In one church I saw the single adult ministry grow from twenty to two hundred in two years! This growth happened because we offered support groups for those dealing with loss through death and divorce. When this ministry happens the church grows to have significant community and kingdom impact.

One of the most beneficial and comprehensive pastoral resources available for church leaders today is the book *Disaster Spiritual Care: Practical Clergy Responses to Community, Regional and National Tragedy* (2017). The updated second edition describes the life cycle of a community disaster and addresses lasting readjustment issues. It describes a number of vital interfaith leadership resources and standards of care that are essential for clergy and caregivers.

I encourage pastors and church leaders to offer recovery groups in their community. You may feel you cannot do one more thing now with all the demands of disaster recovery. If so, plan to offer the recovery group in three to six months. In my personal experience, leading and facilitating a recovery support group is the best thing you can do for yourself and others. Consider using the last six chapters of this book as a small group lesson plan and recovery resource. It is designed to offer personal trauma and financial recovery tools. It is always best to recruit a co-facilitator to work with you in each group. Clergy and other trained caregivers can become facilitators of this six-session program for personal, spiritual, and financial help. By offering scripture-based programs your local church can have much greater community life-enriching impact. Volunteers and victims work together to find recovery opportunities and grow in faith and greater hope. Recovery groups help bring changed lives and offer long-term community impact and transformation.

> "Disaster recovery is in large part the rebuilding of community, the retying of the thousands of strands of relationships that have been severed by the disaster."[10]
>
> —John A. Robinson,
> Presbyterian Disaster Assistance

Consider how your faith community can play a vital role in bringing healing and hope with the good news. Connect with one of many church-related volunteer opportunities. For example, the Texas United Methodist Conference now has three Mission Depots located across the state to provide training, resources, and staging areas for effective disaster relief. During the relief efforts of Hurricane Harvey, which caused flooding of nearly half a million homes, these Mission Depots, their staff, and thousands of volunteers made a real difference.[11]

What can your faith community do? Just do what you can, when you can! Each church can make a difference in disaster relief! Church leaders and staff are aware that more and more people want to serve with significance in mission outreach. Sharing the good news to help disaster victims will bring long-term community transformation. Make each day count for Christ and the church! Helping others through the ministry of the church brings amazing spiritual formation and growth that will continue to bless and impact our world in need!

RECOVERY—
FIVE STEPS FOR TRAUMA
HEALING

There are two basic motivating forces: fear and love....
All hopes for a better world rest in the fearlessness
and open-hearted vision of people who embrace life.

—John Lennon

A very strong wind tore through the mountains and broke apart the stones
before the LORD. But the LORD wasn't in the wind.
After the wind, there was an earthquake.
But the LORD wasn't in the earthquake.
After the earthquake, there was a fire. But the LORD wasn't in the fire.
After the fire, there was a sound. Thin. Quiet.

—1 Kings 19:11-12

Harold Kushner wrote a popular book that was first published in 1981. *When Bad Things Happen to Good People* has brought help to millions of people.[1] His book was the result of his own heartbreak. Harold's three-year-old son was diagnosed with a degenerative disease. His son was not expected to live beyond his early teens. Rabbi Kushner was faced with one of life's most difficult questions: "Why, God?" Maybe you are facing this question too.

I (Clayton) met Rabbi Kushner at a citywide Disaster Recovery Celebration in St. Louis following the great flood of 1992. He was our keynote speaker. During Harold Kushner's introduction, the speaker said, "Rabbi Kushner was correct. We know that bad things happen to good people. They happen to everyone!" We all need help to recover. We would all like to be able to answer the question "Why?"

In a more recent book published in 2015, *Nine Essential Things I've Learned About Life*, Kushner offers even greater understanding in the chapter titled "God Does Not Send the Problem: God Sends Us the Strength to Deal with the Problem."[2] He tells about speaking on the first anniversary of Hurricane Katrina to people in New Orleans's Lower Ninth Ward. He reminds them of the story of Elijah in 1 Kings 19. In this story God was not in the wind, or the earthquake, or the fire. God was in the still small voice. And like Elijah, God's still small voice can give you the courage and determination to recover. Listening to God is a biblical lesson that can help you move forward in faith. However, it is not easy to hear the voice of God.

This chapter is organized around the five essential tasks that can help bring trauma healing. You will also find recovery tools to help you with each of the five tasks. Note that this chapter is written directly to people who have experienced a disaster. For readers who are pastors or other ministry leaders, this chapter functions in the following ways: First, it gives you a foundation for advising and providing help to your congregation or community—or to individuals who've been hit by disaster. The tasks and tools here demonstrate what needs to be done and how to do it. If you are reading this book as *preparation* in case of disaster in your community, this chapter will provide a deeper and more practical understanding.

Second, this material is *immediately useful* for people and communities in the wake of disaster. You may want to share these tasks and tools with people in need right away. This is a nugget of help you can offer *now*. We need trauma-informed care!

Finally, you may be reading this book because you have experienced disaster yourself. In that case, this chapter is designed especially for you. The Bible is full of stories of people who survived disaster. We can learn much—and gain strength—from these stories.

STEP ONE: BEGIN BY SIMPLY COPING

Remember the biblical story of Job? He had a very good life and trusted God completely. But then he experienced disaster after disaster. In spite of this terrible suffering, he deepened his trust in God. Job somehow grew stronger and more resilient. His so-called friends were asking all the wrong questions. When confronted with a disaster, it is important to ask the right questions. The right questions can give direction and take you down the road that leads to recovery. First ask the right questions so that you can better cope with your immediate challenges.

Recovery Tool—Where Can I Go for Help?

Social connections are not just nice to have but are a necessary lifeline at the time of disaster. Help from others can make a significant impact on our health and well-being. Too many times natural disasters result in social isolation. People can lose their sense of belonging.

Contact your family, friends, or church support groups in your neighborhood or area. A faith community can be most helpful,even if you are not a member. Realize that you can find help and you can also help others by getting involved. We are all in this together. We need each other! Joining with others in meaningful activities can create a common purpose. For example, worshiping each week with others like yourself can be uplifting, joyful, and therapeutic.

Recovery Tool—What Do I Do?

Once you make contact with others, be sure to find a time to sit down and begin a conversation. Tell your story. Don't hesitate to tell it again and again. It is very helpful to share your feelings and listen to the feelings of others. This may be a bit difficult at first, but you will feel a sense of relief and find common caring feelings. Writing letters to friends and family members can help you help them. There is something about getting your experience down on paper or in an e-mail that helps you better understand and gain perspective. Get the help you need as soon as you can. If you need professional or pastoral help just ask for it. Find and join a faith-based support group to assist your recovery as soon as possible, or you can begin by utilizing the sessions found in the last six chapters of this book.

Recovery Tool—What Do I Say?

Name what you are feeling daily. Experiencing and expressing your emotions is vital to a healthy recovery. We may feel helpless, powerless, worrisome, distressed, fearful, and angry. Trauma impacts us not only psychologically but also physiologically. Stressful experiences may have an impact on our immune system and make us more vulnerable to illness. Our bodies may be sending physical symptoms of trauma that need attention. Pay attention to what you are feeling. Let your doctor or available health practitioner know if there are health concerns or issues.

In his book *Waking the Tiger: Healing Trauma*, Peter Levin says, "Trauma is a fact of life. It does not, however, have to be a life sentence. How we handle trauma (as individuals, communities, and societies) greatly influences the quality of our lives."[3] Levine goes on to say that trauma may ultimately be recognized as beneficial. Most people can grow through a disaster. When trauma takes place, a transformation may result in an improved quality of life. "While trauma can be hell on earth, trauma (that is) resolved is a gift."[4]

Remind yourself and others that we can learn much about ourselves through our difficulties. Better self-understanding can lead you on a heroic journey of recovery that brings a new life with greater resolve, purpose, and determination. Most people do become stronger and resilient after recovery.

Recovery Tool—Measure Your Stress Level

Track your levels of stress—one to ten with ten being the most stressful. Measure your stress level each morning. Find ways to manage your stress. What brings you comfort? Read and reflect on scriptures that offer peace and calm. Take care of yourself—eat, rest, pray, and exercise daily.

Beware if your stress level reaches nine or ten. Write it down daily. Track your progress. Know that distress is likely an alarm telling you to find professional help, comfort, and care. Know how you are really doing.

STEP TWO: ACCEPT THE REALITY OF LOSS

Acceptance is the doorway we all pass through that leads to greater understanding. Make your grief and mourning matter by being more intentional in what you do and say each day. Give yourself the time you need to pause, think, and pray. Recognize your grief and loss. Healing cannot happen until you accept and understand your loss. Denial delays healing and hope. But also count your blessings. Try to find a balance in your daily life by practicing these tools.

Recovery Tool—Practice Journaling

Starting a journal is a therapeutic way of capturing your thoughts and feelings. As you write you clarify mental confusion or identify other feelings that need expression for healing to begin. Also, your mind will begin to help you take an inventory of your losses caused by the disaster and trauma. Your heart can help you reclaim your blessings and count your gain. Seek a life balance of hope over hurt. Mari L. McCarthy, in her book *Journaling Power*, suggests that it was through journaling that she discovered a door into her soul.[5] Not everyone will want to journal or write a blog, however even a quick list of positive items can be insightful and therapeutic.

Journaling can also include writing down your favorite scriptures, poems, and other quotes. Some people like to draw, take photos, or prepare diagrams to illustrate their journal writings and express themselves. Writing poetry is another creative way of self-discovery and healing. Remember, you do not have to journal daily. You may journal weekly or even monthly. Find an alternate and creative way to express yourself just the way you are. Do what you can, when you can. Make every day count! This Chinese proverb makes a valid point for most: I hear and forget. I see and remember. I write and I understand.

Recovery Tool—Join a Support Group

Recovery support groups can make a positive impact on your healing. My own recovery and healing was enhanced when I become part of a grief recovery group with people who had similar losses. I joined a group of single parents of elementary-age children whose spouse had died. I discovered that others were struggling with similar issues. My perspective and understanding deepened and broadened. I was not the only one in my situation who was wounded and struggling. I was not alone in my pain.

Being part of a faith-based support group helps us recognize the reality of our loss and find companions who share mutual care and concern. The last six chapters of this book offer a small group model that may interest you. There is much common experience to gain from the love and faith of others. You can help start a group that is a great fit for you and your needs, which will also be an opportunity for you to help others with similar interests and needs.

Recovery Tool—Practice Reducing Your Anxiety

Personal meditation can help you when you feel as though you are lost. Sometimes we may feel out of control. Slow down. Pause to recover some control of your surroundings and the awareness of God's care. Pray and meditate on a scripture. For example, here is one of the best:

> I'm not saying this because I need anything, for I have learned how to be content in any circumstance. I know the experience of being in need and of having more than enough; I have learned the secret to being content in any and every circumstance, whether full or hungry or whether having plenty or being poor. I can endure all these things through the power of the one who gives me strength. (Phil 4:11-13)

If personal meditation is new to you, or if it has been awhile since you engaged in this Christian practice, here are some steps that we find helpful:

Begin by breathing slowly—in through your nose; out through your mouth.

Take a look around you: name five things you see; name four things you can touch; name three things you can hear; name two things you can smell; name one emotion you can feel.

Read and reflect on your favorite scriptures.

Pray a prayer of gratitude.

Ask yourself what you can do for others.

Ask yourself what you need from others.

How are we to understand personal anxiety and suffering, especially when we are experiencing it? Often, our pain may block our understanding. Our level of painful feelings may vary from intense to moderate or mild. But whatever the level of pain, it may block our ability to see our situation clearly. And without some understanding it is difficult to find comfort and healing. So what are we to do? There are many great books and resources available; one I recommend is Max Lucado's *Anxious for Nothing: Finding Calm in a Chaotic World.*[6]

Recovery Tool—Diagnosis

When anxiety and suffering is the presenting problem, taking pain medication may only mask the source of pain and suffering. This can compound the problem, and other problems may result. It is vital for disaster victims to take time to study the symptoms and find the necessary help and healing we need. Go to your primary care doctor and find a diagnosis of what is causing the increased level of your suffering. An anti-anxiety medication or an antidepressant may be necessary. Be sure to follow your physician's directions and report back immediately with any negative side effects.

Awareness brings us a step closer to healing and comfort. It is then when we can understand our own unique loss and suffering, and find recovery tools and other ways of treatment that fit us and facilitate a healthy recovery.

I remember my years of playing football. I loved the game and still do. But I am sure some of what my coach said was not that helpful; for example, "No pain, no gain!" Another horse lover and rodeo fan told me a cowboy maxim: "If it hurts, hide it." We need to be aware of our pain. Denial brings long-term suffering. Pain needs our attention and care.

The tyranny of pain and suffering can be overcome if we can identify the cause. Then we get the help we need and may also claim the peace of Christ that passes understanding even in the very midst of life. Through Christian meditation our anxiety can experience a calm that brings emotional and spiritual healing.

STEP THREE: EXPRESS YOUR FEELINGS

During the first year of my grief journey, I did not take enough time for my own healing. I kept very busy caring for my two young children and the congregation I served. I tried to practice good self-care. I journaled, I ran five miles almost daily, I joined a caring grief support group. My prayer life was ongoing, and I had a very supportive family, church family, and close friends. I was doing many things right. At the six-month anniversary of my wife's death, I began to feel more burdened and depressed. I realized that I was now also feeling the impact of loneliness. When I shared this with a close friend, I immediately felt relief.

Recovery Tool—Identify Your Emotions

Depression is as common as having a cold. Anyone may experience symptoms of depression, especially after trauma due to loss. Some may internalize the hurt and anger. Some may feel frozen in fear and feel overwhelmed. This is a sign that we need professional care. When we struggle with our daily responsibilities and relationships, we need to visit a medical doctor or professional counselor. There may be many emotional highs and lows in the journey of recovery. Discern when you need extra help and find the care you need by identifying and expressing your feelings.

I know now that I did not make emotional allowances for what I had lost. Loneliness surprised me with a huge empty feeling. I struggled to express my deep emotion around feeling lonely. It was at the end of my first year of grief that I began to better understand and express my full range of emotions. Praying and talking about my loneliness seemed to have a way of massaging my heartfelt feelings. My emotional well-being was healing from the painful trauma and deep hurt. I could finally feel some inner personal and spiritual healing. The emotional muscles of my heart no longer ached as much.

I realized that I could express my feelings without the intense pain of expression. The more I expressed my feeling, the less pain I experienced. There was less discomfort, and I knew that my heart was healing. I became emotionally and spiritually stronger. I was still on the journey to recovery. I had climbed the mountains of loss and loneliness, and I was making progress.

Recovery Tool—Give Attention to Hurt, Anger, and Fear

Being part of a support group will facilitate a more intentional and sustainable healing process. I first discovered Dr. Howard Clinebell Jr.'s video-based small group program[7] in 1985. I was trying to find healing for my grief and loss from the sudden death of my wife. Like others who experience loss, I was hurt and angry. I joined a Growing through Grief small group. This program was a dynamic healing experience for me and others in my group. Because it helped me so much, I revised this model and facilitated at least forty healing groups over the next fifteen years!

Chapters 7, 8, and 9 of this book offer complimentary small group study plans that offer relief and ways of restoring hope for victims of disaster. These chapters are based on what I have learned and experienced from my studies, clinical training, and four decades of ministry in pastoral care.

It is important for us to explore our hurt, anger, and fear. In most cases hurt is the deepest or core feeling. Reactions to hurt may also be anger and fear. This conversation facilitated a greater understanding of deeper feelings and problems that may prevent healing. We learned that as adults we may have leftover childhood ideas and feelings about God that can cause us to be confused and leave us angry and fearful.

Most of us experience deep hurt at the time of loss and trauma. From the hurt may come anger and fear. Too many times we do not give attention to ways of recognizing anger. Anger and fear are often items of unfinished business. When we live with unresolved anger or fear, we pay a price of diminished aliveness. For example, unresolved anger can lead to depression. We swallow our anger instead of expressing it. You can tell God that you are honestly angry at him! You can find examples of the psalmists who lament and tell God their strongest feelings. God's scripture can and will calm your anger, your pain, and your frustration.

Recovery Tool—Regular Physical Exercise

While spiritual and emotional feelings need to be expressed, it is very important that you consider doing physical exercise regularly. Many people can work out their emotions through physical activity. For example, I reached out to several friends to join me in my favorite sports like racquetball, golf, and running. Your physical condition can actually help improve your emotional and spiritual well-being. Holistic healing involves caring for your body, mind, and soul. Take action. Your self-esteem will be enhanced. Consider getting a trainer to help you develop a tailored exercise workout. Find a walking or running partner. Walk and pray. Find a pace that allows you to get in a breathing and praying rhythm.

STEP FOUR: STRENGTHEN YOUR FAITH

Why do some people stop trusting God and walk away after a significant loss? They may leave the church. They may alienate those they have loved the most in the aftermath of disasters and tragedies. They stop praying and seeking help from others.

People may want to avoid anything that may remind them of their pain and deep hurt. In most cases, people who grieve deeply will adjust to the reality of loss. They recognize that trust in God and friends who care is vital for spiritual recovery. The church may be able to provide a special focus on prayer ministry when people recognize their needs and seek help. One way we can help is by patiently continuing to reach out and pray with those in need.

Recovery Tool—Experience the Power of Prayer

Many people also find great comfort in caring conversations on a regular basis with good friends who offer a confidential ear and nonjudgmental attitude. Setting up regular meetings over coffee or tea can be very helpful. Share your prayer requests. One of my prayer partners would jog with me five days a week. Prayer partners can be most supportive in growing through disaster recovery. If you know of others who, like yourself, would benefit with caring conversation and prayer, start a group.

On Sunday May 22, 2011, disaster struck Joplin, Missouri. Shortly before 5:30 p.m. tornado alarms began to wail. At 5:41 p.m. an F5 tornado cut a path of death and destruction through the middle of the city with a population of over 50,000. It was the deadliest tornado in the United States since 1947. When the storm was over, survivors stood in shock. Their faces revealed the disbelief. Shock soon gave way to trauma and grief. Some asked where God was in this storm. Others just asked why. Eventually, the key question became, "How can God use this suffering to restore and strengthen us?" Community leaders knew a prayer service was needed.

A week later, President Obama visited Joplin and spoke at a prayer and memorial service for the 161 victims. In the weeks to come, church vans and trucks from coast to coast arrived to bring relief to this city of grieving and traumatized people. There were 1,100 people injured, 7,000 homes destroyed, and 300 businesses swept away.

I visited Joplin several times to offer help from our church and share the love of God. A year later, I returned to offer a recovery workshop for church leaders on trauma and grief healing. I heard testimonies of faith about how God especially helped the first emergency responders immediately following the tornado. One first responder said, "It was extremely clear to me that the Lord was guiding us through those first five intense nights and days." Others said, "I heard a still small voice guiding me and directing me every step of the way."

If you visit Joplin today, you will see a beautiful rebuilt city full of faith-filled survivors who have grown more resilient and hopeful. I saw the faith communities reach out with great impact and hope. Pastors I know in the Joplin area tell me that their faith communities practice a vital prayer life. Many continue to experience the power in prayer groups or with a prayer partner.

Recovery Tool—Write Your Personal Lament

Practice reading the many psalms of lament. Psalm 13 is a good example to study. Of the 150 psalms, 67 are considered laments. They describe trauma that is personal and communal. Find a psalm that especially relates to you. Read and reflect on it daily. Write your own lament using a psalm as an example. Structure your lament with this guide:

Address God

Thank God

Offer complaint and feelings

Make confession

Request help

Trust God for help

Offer your praise

Keep your lament in a safe place. Continue to read or pray your lament. Keep revising it. Share it with a positive role model, your recovery group, a prayer partner, or a good friend. I found that when I identified, named, and honored my personal pain I could better acknowledge the pain and enter into it more fully. I could work out that pain like I would work out a sore muscle. Avoiding the pain only made it worse. When one doesn't use physical therapy to work out the muscle soreness of an injured arm, atrophy will occur. That awareness brought relief and greater healing to my grief and trauma wounds. Laments can actually bring help and healing to our souls.

STEP FIVE: HELPING OTHERS HELPS YOURSELF

Overcoming trauma and grief is difficult work. It takes time and requires your action. It can be a faith journey for you to go through and experience healing of your trauma wounds. The good news is that you can grow through your grief to become stronger and more resilient. As I began to help others, I immediately realized that by helping others I, too, was being helped.

Recovery Tool—Seek the Best Help

I discovered that I was not alone in my trauma when I joined a grief support group with other parents of school-age children who had lost a spouse. At the end of that six-week group session, the group leader asked me to facilitate the next support group. Not only can you help yourself, but you can help others grow closer to God, family, and friends.

Let me offer a helpful and practical suggestion that I learned in seminary. David Switzer, my professor of pastoral care at Perkins School of Theology, wrote one of the best books on the subject of grief, called *The Dynamics of Grief.*[8] My suggestion, when you are emotionally ready, is to research your symptoms of grief and trauma. I drove over one thousand miles to visit with my former seminary mentors and professors, which made all the difference to me. Find the best help you can.

Begin your recovery journey with the end in mind. I wanted to become a better father to my young children. I wanted to become a better pastor to my congregation. Visualize the person you want to become. Find the best help and take action to be the best you can be.

Recovery Tool—Find Positive Role Models

We especially need positive role models. Seek out a person or two who has experienced a similar loss. Listen to their story. How did they cope? Where is the source of their hope? Be a good listener. Take notes if that helps you. You can learn from others' successes and setbacks. You will realize that you are not the only person dealing with doubt, fear, anger, and many other strong feelings. You can learn from others new ways to answer your most difficult questions.

Find a positive role model who listens well. You can express your thoughts and emotions. Identify your emotions and the questions they raise. Consider speaking to these key questions to facilitate your process of healing: What happened? How did you feel immediately? What is the hardest part for you? What resources are now available to help you?

We will get relief, even if it is temporary, by sharing our pain and the flow of tears. As we find the help we need from others who will listen to us, we will then be better to help others. I found that I was at my best when I recognized that because I had been helped I could become a "wounded healer." We may develop a passion and faith perspective to help others as we have been helped.

Recovery Tool—Share God's Mercy

Some of the wisest people I have known over the years are those who have known loss, suffering, and struggle. But by God's mercy and grace they have found their way out of the pit of despair. In their loss they discovered a greater gain. Their pain and emptiness have been replaced with compassion, concern, and greater caring for others in need. Is there anything more powerful than the redemption and restoration power of God?

The most important commandments of the scriptures are to love God and to love others as you love yourself. This is the foundation of faith upon which you can rebuild your new life. So many times trauma knocks us down and we feel so unworthy and inadequate. We can relearn the value of loving ourselves and loving others through the power of Christ's amazing grace. I have seen too many people give up on love because it hurts to love when there is traumatic loss. The truth is that love matters more when we need it the most. Love is eternal, and nothing can separate us from the love of God through the saving work of Christ on the cross.

As we learn to better love and care for ourselves, we are then better able to love and care for others. We can sense the Holy Spirit counseling us to offer more love and compassion. Mercy becomes contagious. The more we give of ourselves, the more we receive and the sooner we become the new person we want to become. Romans 8:35-39 offers an amazing reassurance that nothing can separate us from God's love.

> Who will separate us from Christ's love? Will we be separated by trouble, or distress, or harassment, or famine, or nakedness, or danger, or sword? As it is written,
>
> We are being put to death all day long for your sake.
>
> We are treated like sheep for slaughter.
>
> But in all these things we win a sweeping victory through the one who loved us. I'm convinced that nothing can separate us from God's love in Christ Jesus our Lord: not death or life, not angels or rulers, not present things or future things, not powers or height or depth, or any other thing that is created.

We want to act in such a way that we are a reflection of a loving and merciful God.

It is the power of this love that gives us the strength we need to let go of our grief. And by "letting go" of the painful, traumatic memories of loss, we find room for good grief filled with a legacy of love. We can let go of the pain and the depression, and experience a sense of healing and hope. Because we have found that mercy, healing, and hope, we want to help others. Martin Luther King Jr. emphasized that the most important question in life is, "What are you doing for others?"

Recovery Tool—Take a Self-Inventory

In chapter 3 we are going to focus on ways we can reignite hope that will help bring renewal and restore your life. With extreme loss and life change come many challenges and even greater opportunities. Check off the following areas that you need to continue working on as you seek to grow and find healing:

_____ Realize that recovery is hard work. (Job 36:15)

_____ Find a disaster recovery group that can help you and others. (Eccl 7:12)

_____ Learn more about the dynamics and symptoms of trauma and grief. (Job 36:15)

_____ Continue to accept the reality of your loss. (Ps 31:9)

_____ Seek trust in God and daily practice your faith disciplines. (Isa 53:4-6)

_____ Learn from positive role models and other communities who have experienced similar trauma and loss. (John 8:32)

_____ Recognize and overcome obstacles to your recovery and find the help you need. (Heb 4:16)

_____ Picture or visualize a healthier and happier future. Meditate on the truth of scripture. (Heb 4:12)

_____ Remember the good; say good-bye to the pain and lingering trauma. (Lam 3:32)

_____ Express and experience your emotions and feel the relief and new understanding. (Ps 102:1)

_____ Write your own personal lament using Psalm 22 as an example. (Isa 30:8)

_____ Realize that recovery means you say goodbye to your losses but remember those you love. (Rev 4:9)

Each of us may experience trauma, loss, and grief differently. Each of us is unique in the way we understand and express our emotions. Growth through disaster comes through the transformation of God's healing in ways that will define us and our future.

Chapter 3

RESTORATION— REIGNITING HOPE

As the Father loved me, I too have loved you. Remain in my love.
If you keep my commandments, you will remain in my love,
just as I kept my Father's commandments and remain in his love.
I have said these things to you so that my joy will be in you
and your joy will be complete.
This is my commandment: love each other just as I have loved you.
—John 15:9-12

Hope begins in the dark, the stubborn hope that if you just show up
and try to do the right thing, the dawn will come.
You wait and watch and work; you don't give up.[1]
—Anne Lamott

Hope is God's powerful gift of love for us that offers us a future with confidence and assurance. How would you define hope? For most, our hope is diminished in the aftermath of a disaster. Reigniting hope is the spark of love that we need to begin our journey of recovery. Hope offers us a most powerful blessing to do the impossible.

The city of Joplin, Missouri, was devastated by a F5 tornado on May 22, 2011. Renee White served as the chairperson of the Joplin Long-Term Recovery Committee. In the post-disaster book *Joplin Pays It Forward*, she writes about the vital need for long-term restoration:

This Blessing has guided me throughout the past 22 months. It conveys my deepest beliefs about the work we have accomplished. (The blessing is from an anonymous author.)

*May you be blessed with a restless discomfort about easy answers,
half-truths and superficial relationships, so that you may live deep
within your heart.*

*May you be blessed with anger at injustice, oppression, and
exploitation of people, so that you may tirelessly work for justice,
freedom, and peace.*

*May you be blessed with the gift of tears to shed with those
who suffer from pain, rejection, starvation, or the loss of all
that they cherish, so that you may reach out your hand
to comfort them and transform their pain into joy.*

*And, may you be blessed with enough hope to believe that
you really can make a difference in this world, so that you can do
what others claim cannot be done.*[2]

This chapter invites you to claim an increased hope that is often diminished during times of disaster. The tools we share are based on the power of God's love to reignite diminished hope. Like the previous chapter, it is written for both victims, leaders, and caregivers. If you are a leader or caregiver, this material is further preparation for you. It is also immediately sharable, a way to help *now*. If you are a person who is experiencing disaster, this chapter can guide you on a pathway to hope. This faith-based approach will assist leaders and members of local churches and faith communities in long-term restoration and resilience.

Trauma and the reality of personal loss can create obstacles to our hope for recovery and God's grace. Immediately after disaster strikes, victims are shocked, stunned, and numb. Our homes and churches are devastated or damaged. More immediate physical and medical needs must be addressed. Health problems may be acute and need urgent care. Children and youth especially need reassurance and security. Feelings of isolation set in for all age levels. Unfortunately, too many withdraw from the support we need.

In many cases, survivors of the disaster may take months or years to get their lives back to a new normal. They must take one step, one hour, one day at a time. Victims slowly set up a new routine to help organize their lives. They do whatever they can do. Each day may get better as they seek a new normal.

Adjustments come slowly as life has changed. Accepting the reality of loss and change brings new concerns and questions. We hear people say, "I will always be afraid." Unhealthy thoughts of never-ending fear can be replaced with more hope-filled expressions such as, "I was fearful and now my fears have lessened." Some people avoid talking about their feelings. Others feel that in time their fears will go away. One pastor said, "Time alone can put scabs on wounds and ferment wine, but it does not heal grief." Growing through disaster takes work. We all need inspirational motivation to overcome the obstacle of fear. In Adam Hamilton's book *Unafraid*, he reminds us that when we face our fears with faith we are starting with our bias of hope...a hope-filled faith. Hope happens when nothing else will![3]

The new normal becomes more evident after the first six to twelve months. Survivors begin to rediscover the power of hope that helps them begin to resolve their grief, loss, and trauma. Remember the words of the old spiritual:

It's so high you can't get over it
It's so low you can't get under it
It's so wide you can't get around it
You must go through the door!

In *Life after Loss*, pastor Bob Deits writes, "To go through grief is the only lasting way out of grief."[4]

Years ago, Dr. Glen Davidson, founding chair of the medical department at Southern Illinois University, was invited to speak at my church to a large group of pastors. He made a lasting impression on me about health care issues. He had researched the health dangers of unresolved grief and trauma. His research work demonstrated that nearly 25 percent of those who mourn experience a dramatic decrease in their body's immune system six to nine months after their loss.[5] This is why people can develop life-threatening illnesses within a year after serious trauma, because of dehydration and other complications. He taught that drinking more water and a following a nutritious diet is essential, especially for those dealing with grief and trauma. Regular exercise is also very important.

This chapter identifies the attributes of God's love that can inform and inspire ways to reignite hope in your life. God's love and hope help us conquer our fears. Pick one or more of these biblical attributes that fits your needs now. Many must rebuild their homes after a disaster. All of us must rebuild or restore our diminished hope. God offers hope.

Begin with the end in mind. What do you want your future to look like? People today may need more than one to two years for the pain and fears to diminish so that life is more hopeful, manageable, and meaningful. Patience prevails and allows healthy healing. Hope, no matter how small, will ignite greater faith in God, self-love, and love of others. Paul writes in 1 Corinthians 13:7: "Love puts up with all things, trusts in all things, hopes for all things, endures all things."

Scripture can help support and anchor your hope. There are over three hundred references to *hope* in our Bible. For people of faith, one of the best strategies for hope can be found in scripture. If you do not already have a hope-focused scripture, find one that speaks to you and memorize it. Your hope will grow as you pray this scripture in times of need.

Our belief system is essential for our disaster recovery. Social ties that connect us to our faith community are built on love of neighbor and God. Howard Clinebell Jr., who has written several books on grief, said, "A healthy religious faith and support of a spiritual community have the unique ability to help turn miserable minuses into positive pluses."[6]

Hope helps each of us, regardless of our age, in many unique and strategic ways:

Hope broadens and deepens our experience and view of life.

Hope offers motivation to recover.

Hope provides an antidote to frustration.

Hope carries us out of despair and loneliness.

Hope brings strength in spite of our weakness.

Hope gives birth to our assurance of eternal love.

Hope can be for you the highest expression of spiritual, emotional, and intellectual life.

Hope becomes life itself. Hope awakens us.

Hope gives us energy.

Hope is wonder.

Whenever we feel discouraged, especially when we feel despair over some misdeed in our life, we can immediately remember hope: that God is always waiting for us with unconditional love. God relates to us in the present moment, not in the past or future!

Trauma brings us feelings of being powerless and out of control. We only see our helplessness and limits. Trauma can be one of the most acute and chronic forms of suffering that anyone can experience. Hope is something we can hold on to as we walk through our crises. Any time we begin to feel fear, we must remember to reach out to trust God's hope. I invite you to consider these tools to reignite your hope.

THE CROSS—GOD'S STRATEGY OF HOPE

The cross bore the suffering and trauma of Jesus. It has the power to teach us that our suffering is not just our own. God suffers with us in a mystery of grace. Out of the passion the cross becomes a symbol of hope. Hope was reignited after the resurrection of Jesus Christ. The cross points to how God can use tragedy, suffering, betrayal, pain, and even death. And the empty cross powerfully symbolizes that there is hope beyond trauma. We can trust in God's strategy of the empty cross—that our life and death be not in vain.

Our pain, like the pain of Jesus upon the cross, is not God's way of punishing us. Our suffering, like the suffering of Christ, offers a way God can bring us closer to the meaning and purpose of our true spiritual salvation of hope. The Gospels offer seven sayings of Jesus at the time of his crucifixion trauma. These were not words of defeat. These sayings bear witness to the power of hope. Jesus experienced distress, abandonment, and suffering. In his suffering, our suffering can find ultimate meaning in the hope of the empty cross.

Reigniting Tool—Trust God

Trust is the first and most important spiritual foundation for your recovery. An abiding trust in God leads to hope. It is in that trust that we can decide to begin to seek a deeper love for life itself. This journey is best when it is intentional. Make the decision to grow through your loss and experience healing as soon as you are ready to trust God. Remember, love is a decision. Do not hesitate too long, but be prayerful and intentional in your decision.

God's love is the greatest *moving power of life*. Only love has the power to restore us from times of disaster, grief, and loss. Paul writes, "We know that in all things God works for the good of those who love him" (Rom 8:28, NIV). We know that trauma, grief, and loss are an inevitable part of disaster. Love reminds us that God is with us. We can identify with our suffering with the suffering of Christ. Our suffering gets God's attention. C. S. Lewis wrote that "God whispers to us in our pleasures, speaks in our conscience, but shouts in our pain."[7] God's love is the greatest because it is the powerful source of faith and hope!

The truth is that we often first seek God in times of need. Proverbs 20:30 says, "Sometimes it takes a painful experience to make us change our ways" (GNT). Human as we are, we often take God's love for granted. However, when we put our hope in God's love, we can strengthen and grow our character. As simple and as sentimental as this love sounds, love does help us rebuild our lives. Love is the foundation upon which our personal and spiritual restoration can be rebuilt. Philosopher and theologian Pierre Teilhard de Chardin expressed his vision of the power of love:

> Love alone is capable of uniting living beings in such a way as to complete and fulfill them, for it alone takes them and joins them by what is deepest in them. This is a

fact of daily experience....And if that is what it can achieve daily on a small scale, why should it not repeat this one day on world-wide dimensions?[8]

Reigniting Tool—Search for Meaning in Suffering

Our suffering matters to God. Do you ever wonder why we suffer? Does God cause our suffering, or is suffering just part of life? Is suffering a consequence of our free will? In our struggle to understand suffering, we can begin to discover the restoration of meaning and our purpose in life. God does not cause us to suffer. However, God can help us use our suffering to prepare us for eternity. If we were to paraphrase 2 Corinthians 4:17-18, it would read, "These little troubles are getting us ready for an eternal glory that will make all our trouble seem like nothing. Things that are seen don't last forever, but things that are not seen are eternal. That's why we keep our minds on the things that cannot be seen."

History teaches us that wisdom comes from those who have survived great trauma. Rabbi Harold Kushner learned from Victor Frankl (1905–1997), who survived the Holocaust and became a trusted psychiatrist. Kushner was invited to write the foreword to a 2006 reprint of Frankl's seminal book *Man's Search for Meaning*, and underscore's Frankl's own words:

> Frankl's most enduring insight, one that I have called on often in my own life and in countless counseling situations: "Forces beyond your control can take away everything you possess except one thing, your freedom to choose how you will respond to the situation. You cannot control what happens to you in life, but you can always control what you will feel and do about what happens to you."[9]

Well-known ecumenical author Richard Rohr, who also serves as director of the Center for Action and Contemplation, tells the story of another Holocaust victim who died at Auschwitz. In her journal on June 15, 1941, she wrote,

> For a moment yesterday I thought I could not go on living, that I needed help. Life and suffering had lost their meaning to me; I felt I was about to collapse....I feel like a small battlefield, in which the problems of our time are being fought out. All one can hope to do is to keep oneself humbly available, to allow oneself to be a battlefield.[10]

Reigniting Tool—Ask God for Help

If we trust God and believe that God can help us use our suffering for good, then it is time to ask God for help. To do this we must be in touch with our real feelings. It is true that our feelings may get tangled up in our suffering. Our tangled feelings become like a logjam on an icy river. Our life energy cannot flow except with help from a greater force than ourselves. It is also true that we get all tangled up and confused in our search for God's love; and the truth is we do not realize that the root of suffering is based on the deprivation of love. What obstacle are you dealing with that may be causing the logjam or blocking your connection to the love of God? What is separating you from God's grace?

We all need quiet time—time to sort out and get in touch with our thoughts, feelings, and soul. It is in these quiet moments that we find God is in control of all that really matters. Five minutes a day with God can make a difference in eternity. Psalm 46:10 (NIV) puts it this way: "Be still, and know that I am God."

Howard Thurman, a well-known theologian and civil rights leader, once described how each of us, through contemplation, can approach God:

> There is in every person an inward sea, and in that sea there is an island and on that island there is an altar. And standing guard before that altar is the "angel with the flaming sword." Nothing can get by that angel to be placed upon that altar unless it has the mark of your inner authority. Nothing passes...unless it be a part of the fluid area of your consent. This is your crucial link with the eternal.[11]

The intentional practice of prayer helps us express ourselves in ways that bring clarity, truth, and understanding of our thoughts and feelings. This spiritual practice can help you look within yourself and discover those places that are blocking your view as you seek God's healing. Begin to write out your prayers. As you seek God you can better experience an immense tenderness and understanding of God's love.

We all ask, "Why are there disasters?" The urgency of this question reminds us that we may never find the answers. However, we never stop asking the question and seeking the answers. We find comfort when others join us on our search together. Finally, we realize that we may not ever get the answers we seek. However, we can ask a better question: "What can we do about this disaster?" We discover what we can do, and then we do it. We accept our absolute dependence upon God. By faith, we can and do trust in God's grace. We believe in Christ, who is the way, the truth, and the life (John 14:6). As our faith seeks understanding, I believe we can be awed by the glory of God ahead of us as we seek the way, the truth, and the life eternal and your fears will fall behind us.

Reigniting Tool—Accept the Healing Power of Love

Sometimes each one of us will ask ourselves, *What is wrong with me?* Rather, first ask, *What has happened to me?* Trauma happens to everyone. We jump to conclusions and think something must be wrong with ourselves. But sometimes we have been traumatized and we do not recognize what has happened to us. We may be numb. We may be in shock. We may be in denial. We can make every effort to forget or cover up our pain. In doing this we may compound our pain and suffering. Begin to believe that God's love is sufficient.

What really happens to us at a time of trauma, and why is trauma healing so important? Trauma causes a feeling of powerless. We cannot control or protect ourselves from that which is about to cause pain, or may already be inflicting pain, serious harm, or even death. Trauma is an acute form of suffering, and we feel most helpless. Trauma can also become chronic. When it does, it destroys our lives. Not only can trauma impact individuals, but it can impact families, churches, communities, and even nations.

Here is what I know and trust: Love does not protect us. Yet love sustains us. Love brings healing in a slow act of transformation. We can depend upon God's healing love. When we trust in God's healing power, we experience the peace of God that surpasses our understanding.

Rohr offers this hope:

> The genius of Jesus' ministry is that he reveals how God uses tragedy, suffering, pain, betrayal, and death itself (all of which are normally inevitable), not to punish us but, in fact, to bring us to God and to our True Self, which are frequently discovered simultaneously. There are no dead ends in this spiritual life. Nothing is above or beyond redemption. Everything (including disaster) can be used for transformation.[12]

Reigniting Tool—Love Hopes

This is the best part of love. Love hopes. Love invites us to journey with hope. This hope-filled love will not let us go! We may wonder if we are going to survive in the midst of a disaster. We feel painful waves of fear washing over us, blowing us away, or shaking the ground we stand on. We trust that God will sustain us with hope so that our fear doesn't cause us to freeze or be overcome in panic. When we trust God in the storm, we act in faith to save ourselves and others. Our love for God helps us be our best in the times that are our worst and we are most vulnerable. Through hope we develop resilience, which will continue to sustain us in future traumatic events and trials.

In the storms of life we need a hope we can trust. Bruce Blumer's book *Simply Grace* shares the story of his daughter's illness and death. We may identify with his powerful words: "When I was at my most vulnerable, my raw and naked, my most helpless—that was when I was truly able to know God, to learn to trust him and to fully experience his power, his love, his faithfulness, and his grace."[13]

Reigniting Tool—Act with Hope

The more you put your hope in God, the more healing happens. Your journey continues at the cross of Christ. You begin to realize that your suffering matters in ways that give new meaning and purpose for life. Daily ask for God's love and daily claim the power of that love that bears, believes, hopes, and endures all things. Recognize and believe that this love is the balm that heals your trauma and grief wounds. Celebrate a love that reignites new hope and new life through Christ. And finally, you can witness and act with the assurance of hope that nothing can separate you from the eternal love of God.

Dr. Howard Clinebell Jr. tells this closing story about a woman of faith and hope:

> When Clem's little daughter, Ruth, died on her first birthday, the whole family was shattered by the tragedy. With intuitive awareness, Clem knew that she must be something to bear the crushing load of grief. Her response was an expression of her deep faith.
>
> For several years she watched her hometown paper carefully. When we read of the death of a child, she wrote a brief note to the parents saying very simply how sorry she was, that they were in her prayers, and that she knew something about the dark valley through which they were walking. She, too, had lost a dear child.
>
> Clem never discussed how much the grieving parents to whom she wrote were helped. But it is Clem, herself, who found deep healing in sending those little notes.
>
> She felt she was responding to God's intention for her life in those dark days. I am profoundly grateful for Clem's example. Clem Lucille Clinebell was my mother.[14]

Clem sets an example for us in her legacy of faith, hope, and love! What is your intentional action plan for recovery and restoration? When we go through a disaster, we need an action plan for good mental and spiritual health that includes what we can do for others. Faith makes all things possible, but never easy. Remember the encouraging words from 1 Chronicles 28:20: "Be strong and courageous....Get to work. Don't be afraid or discouraged, because the LORD, my God, is with you. He will never let you down or leave you."

Every generation is in need of encouraging hope that ignites action. I invite you to follow these closing words of action attributed to Dr. Martin Luther King Jr.:

If you can't run then walk,

If you can't walk then crawl.

But whatever you do you have to keep moving forward!

PART II

FINANCIAL FOUNDATIONS AND RECOVERY

*Rock bottom became the solid foundation on
which I rebuilt my life.*[1]

—J. K. Rowling

No one in my family can understand how I (Matt) cannot be a Harry Potter fan. I'm sorry, but I'm just more of a C. S. Lewis and J. R. R. Tolkien kind of guy. However, the above quote attributed to Harry Potter author, J. K. Rowling, is one I absolutely admire. How can you not respect her raw honesty and singular focus? Hundreds of publishers rejected Rowling's Potter manuscript. (What were those guys thinking?) I may not be a fan of the story myself, but I am totally impressed by her never-say-die attitude and the guts she had to keep trying in the face of so much failure and rejection.

As we begin looking at the topic of financial recovery in Part II of *Growing through Disaster*, you very well may need the perseverance exhibited by Rowling to meet the trauma challenge you face. Being a Chicagoan, I've never been one to pull punches. Recovery is hard work, be it emotional, physical, or financial. In this section, I will shoot straight while providing practical tools to help you begin your financial recovery. Additionally, I aim to offer encouragement and spiritual insight into how God is at your side, wanting to help you in this critical area. In my financial ministry, I find most people lack a framework or system for money management; therefore, I will provide tips and ideas to try to make the recovery process as easy as possible. I will help you build a firm financial foundation and a simple plan to begin your financial recovery.

In chapter 4, "Assessment: Taking Your Financial Pulse," you will take a financial check-up quiz that will help you identify areas of your personal finances that need the most immediate attention, determine areas of strength and weakness, and allow you to begin prioritizing the steps of your recovery plan. Realizing that you must first make an assessment of your current situation before you can move forward, I will guide you through some simple checklists and exercises to help you know where to start. Frankly, this is sometimes the most difficult hurdle to overcome. Once you see where you stand, it is far easier to begin taking steps toward your goals. After reading this chapter, the corresponding small group in chapter 7 will aid you in setting those goals you need to lead you to recovery.

40

Chapter 5, "Spending Plan: Money Management Strategies," will introduce five core biblical principles that will form a solid foundation for how to manage your finances. By employing these five common-sense values into your financial dealings, they will both aid you while working through the recovery phase and become lifelong guideposts to sound fiscal management. We will explore how giving can be a conduit to recovery and generosity. The principle of generous giving will also lead you toward the second step of fleeing the love of money. Principles three through five begin to move into the more practical realm of money management, where you will see how scripture guides us to live within our means, plan for the future, and use a spending plan (not a budget!) to find success in our monthly financial dealings.

Finally, in chapter 6, "Planning: Your Financial Recovery Plan," we will dig even deeper into the area of planning. Our focus will be to help you build immediate, intermediate, and long-term financial recovery plans that are simple, have manageable steps, and will motivate you to keep rebuilding your life. Once your personal recovery plan is built, we will begin to look forward to other planning steps that will help in case another financial disaster threatens you. While we cannot insulate ourselves from all risk, having a grab and go emergency kit will help you have your key financial and legal information at your fingertips, should an emergency arise. To wrap up the chapter, we provide a brief overview of what I call "legacy of love" planning. We will explore the benefits and differences of having a will or a trust, as well as seven critical legal documents that every one of us needs to protect ourselves and our families.

At the end of Part II, you will have a practical action plan in place to begin healing in your financial world. Simple and practical tools, exercises, and checklists are the hallmark of this section. Thomas Edison once said, "Most people miss opportunity because it's dressed in overalls and looks like work." If you employ a modicum of Edison-inspired effort, receive encouragement and direction from your small group leaders, and combine it with some Rowling-like chutzpah, we are certain the financial recovery section of *Growing through Disaster* can set you on a path of positive momentum to financial restoration from your current setback.

Chapter 4

ASSESSMENT— TAKING YOUR FINANCIAL PULSE

Where your treasure is, there your heart will be also.
—Matthew 6:21

Awareness is the first step to progress.[1]
—The Power of Focus

I t is somewhat comical, really, for me (Matt) to admit how much of my general knowledge of life has come from TV, movies, and song lyrics. However, the reality is you can learn a lot about many topics if you observe closely. For instance, I never would have known what a Hasselblad was without the Larry Norman song "I Am the Six O'clock News" (it is a high-quality camera); and though I possess absolutely zero medical background or training, I know a lot about triage from watching the 1970's hit comedy-drama TV show *M*A*S*H* ("Mobile Army Surgical Hospital," for the younger crowd). Medical triage is the process where the doctors and nurses make a quick assessment of a patient or group of patients to determine which people have the highest priority need for medical care. The more serious the wound or condition, the faster the injured party gets treatment.

If you have experienced a financial trauma of any sort, you are likely in need of immediate financial triage. Even if the event occurred weeks or months ago, we need to take a quick assessment to help determine what needs to be done first. Our objective in this chapter will be crisis intervention, a quick, effective triage process, followed by a swift patch up to your wallet so that more attention can be given to your financial health down the line at a "money hospital" (e.g., a local church financial class). The small group sessions in this book could also be a logical place to help you start rebuilding.

I will introduce a practical assessment tool to help you determine exactly where you stand financially after the crisis you have faced. No doubt what you have experienced is quite overwhelming. We aim to help you focus and begin to formulate your plan. Whether you are coming out of a divorce, or if your house was rocked by an earthquake, my financial triage tool will help you assess your condition and then point out the actions to take to stop the immediate fiscal bleeding. I think even *M*A*S*H* doctor Hawkeye Pierce would approve.

LESSONS FROM THE PAST

Anne, who you will meet when she shares her story in chapter 10, experienced the financial trauma of divorce. She shares this sage advice for helping you as you rebuild your financial world:

> Learn to manage the emotions and fear that come with trauma. Emotions unchecked can undue you and make you burn energy, waste money, and lose focus.

> What seems like a huge deal at the time of the trauma can often be an emotional trap. Stay true to your values and top priorities (no matter the type of trauma) and don't fall prey to emotional manipulations or distractions. (Deal with these in your small group or in counseling.)

> If dealing with divorce, refuse to badmouth your ex to your kids. Take the high road and honor your ex. Pray for those who oppose you to break the cycle of dysfunction.

> Focus on the end game of what you are trying to accomplish and not having to be "right." These strategies will lessen your stress and trauma.

Let's start like any good triage process and take your financial vital signs. It will be imperative to take your financial pulse so that you can decide which areas of your situation you must address first. Once you have dealt initially with the grief and shock of the crisis (which Clayton has addressed for us in chapter two), you will want to consider the following to get back on your feet:

- How much cash do I have on hand?

- Do I have access to any of my key financial tools: checkbook, debit or credit cards, personal records or documentation (social security card, insurance policies, and safe-deposit box key)?

- Do I have all the financial/legal information and documents I will need to rebuild? Do I have an organizer to house all this information?

- Does my job have a disaster response plan? Do I have a copy? What are my work responsibilities if there is a disaster?

- Do I have any items of value I could use for barter if necessary?

- Will credit or debit cards work, or are there electronic systems in place to be able to process payments? If not, cash will truly be king.

The simple quote that opened this chapter, taken from the book *The Power of Focus,* is a lifelong favorite: "Awareness is the first step to progress." The following financial checkup quiz is designed to help you take an assessment of your current financial situation and determine which areas you need to focus on first to begin your recovery. We know this can be a very scary step, because no matter what financial trauma you have experienced, it can feel completely overwhelming. However, the reality is we must begin to dig out.

I have been a financial coach for nearly twenty-five years, yet, I am still surprised on a regular basis how often people have no idea what is going on with their finances, such an integral part of life. In my experience, I find that the situation is rarely as bad as the person thinks it is, once we finally get their information out in the open and down on paper. Once the *awareness* part of the process commences, and we put pencil to paper, we can record key financial information to get a basic understanding of one's situation. It is astounding the amount of hope and positive energy that is generated by the simple step of writing it down. As you begin to take stock of your situation, these small steps almost always help you begin to move forward. Ephesians 5:13-14 states, "But everything exposed by the light becomes visible—and everything that is illuminated becomes a light. This is why it is said: 'Wake up, sleeper, rise from the dead, and Christ will shine on you'" (NIV).

> We welcome the Holy Spirit to illuminate our financial world as well.

The numbing effect that comes from trauma also impacts our finances. As we expose this part of our life to the light of Christ, we welcome in the Holy Spirit to illuminate our financial world as well. The sleeper will rise, the numbing spell of trauma will be broken, and you will begin on the road to repairing your financial world.

FINANCIAL CHECKUP QUIZ

Your scores in each area will be used to help you determine what action to take to improve your situation if needed. Based on the statements listed below, rate yourself on a scale from 1 to 10. This scale will help you understand how to gauge your rating:

1	2	3	4	5	6	7	8	9	10

Always describes   **Sometimes describes**   **Never describes**
your situation   **your situation**   **your situation**

Based on how you score, it will also begin to provide you with an idea of specific actions you can take to strengthen your financial situation.

Income and Money Management

1. I have income that will continue during this crisis to meet my basic needs.

1	2	3	4	5	6	7	8	9	10

Always describes   **Sometimes describes**   **Never describes**
your situation   **your situation**   **your situation**

2. I have funds set aside that I can access immediately to handle emergency costs of living.

1	2	3	4	5	6	7	8	9	10

Always describes   **Sometimes describes**   **Never describes**
your situation   **your situation**   **your situation**

3. I have developed a written week-to-week spending plan to cover my basic living needs during the crisis

1	2	3	4	5	6	7	8	9	10

Always describes   **Sometimes describes**   **Never describes**
your situation   **your situation**   **your situation**

4. I know my key account numbers (bank, savings, and investment).

| 1 | 2 | 3 | 4 | 5 | 6 | 7 | 8 | 9 | 10 |

Always describes your situation   **Sometimes describes your situation**   **Never describes your situation**

5. I have access to cash for day-to-day spending needs during the crisis.

| 1 | 2 | 3 | 4 | 5 | 6 | 7 | 8 | 9 | 10 |

Always describes your situation   **Sometimes describes your situation**   **Never describes your situation**

Insurance and Relief Resources

1. I am aware of my insurance coverages and options.

| 1 | 2 | 3 | 4 | 5 | 6 | 7 | 8 | 9 | 10 |

Always describes your situation   **Sometimes describes your situation**   **Never describes your situation**

2. I have been in contact with my insurance agent/company about my situation.

| 1 | 2 | 3 | 4 | 5 | 6 | 7 | 8 | 9 | 10 |

Always describes your situation   **Sometimes describes your situation**   **Never describes your situation**

3. I am aware of any government resources that can provide me with immediate assistance.

| 1 | 2 | 3 | 4 | 5 | 6 | 7 | 8 | 9 | 10 |

Always describes your situation   **Sometimes describes your situation**   **Never describes your situation**

4. I have explored other relief resources from my church or other national organizations.

1	2	3	4	5	6	7	8	9	10

Always describes your situation   **Sometimes describes your situation**   **Never describes your situation**

5. I have a plan of how to best use insurance/relief proceeds I receive.

1	2	3	4	5	6	7	8	9	10

Always describes your situation   **Sometimes describes your situation**   **Never describes your situation**

Debts and Obligations

1. I have communicated with my credit card company and worked out a payment plan in light of this financial crisis (also for auto loans, school loans, or personal loans).

1	2	3	4	5	6	7	8	9	10

Always describes your situation   **Sometimes describes your situation**   **Never describes your situation**

2. I am paying my bills on time.

1	2	3	4	5	6	7	8	9	10

Always describes your situation   **Sometimes describes your situation**   **Never describes your situation**

3. I have a plan in place regarding any reoccurring electronic bill payments to ensure the funds will be there to cover the costs (suspend or cancel plan if needed based on your type of financial trauma).

1	2	3	4	5	6	7	8	9	10

Always describes your situation   **Sometimes describes your situation**   **Never describes your situation**

4. I have contacted the utility companies regarding any change/suspension of service in relation to my financial crisis.

1	2	3	4	5	6	7	8	9	10

**Always describes   Sometimes describes   Never describes
your situation   your situation   your situation**

5. My debts and bills are under control.

1	2	3	4	5	6	7	8	9	10

**Always describes   Sometimes describes   Never describes
your situation   your situation   your situation**

Long-Range Financial Planning

1. I have secured lodging for the next three to six months (or more if needed) to get me through this crisis situation.

1	2	3	4	5	6	7	8	9	10

**Always describes   Sometimes describes   Never describes
your situation   your situation   your situation**

2. I will have adequate income for the next three to six months.

1	2	3	4	5	6	7	8	9	10

**Always describes   Sometimes describes   Never describes
your situation   your situation   your situation**

3. I have mapped out a plan to cover basic living expenses for the next three to six months.

1	2	3	4	5	6	7	8	9	10

**Always describes   Sometimes describes   Never describes
your situation   your situation   your situation**

4. I have written out a list of my assets and debts to help me assess my options for covering expenses and debts in the coming months.

1	2	3	4	5	6	7	8	9	10

   Always describes   **Sometimes describes**   **Never describes**
     your situation   **your situation**   **your situation**

5. I am committed to saving money each month to begin building/replenishing my emergency fund.

1	2	3	4	5	6	7	8	9	10

   Always describes   **Sometimes describes**   **Never describes**
     your situation   **your situation**   **your situation**

Giving Plan

1. Even in the midst of this setback, I am regularly giving back to others who may be even worse off than myself.

1	2	3	4	5	6	7	8	9	10

   Always describes   **Sometimes describes**   **Never describes**
     your situation   **your situation**   **your situation**

2. I believe the money and resources in my possession belong to God, and I just manage what he has given to me, no matter how much or how little I have.

1	2	3	4	5	6	7	8	9	10

   Always describes   **Sometimes describes**   **Never describes**
     your situation   **your situation**   **your situation**

3. I am able to give money to God's work with a cheerful heart.

1	2	3	4	5	6	7	8	9	10

   Always describes   **Sometimes describes**   **Never describes**
     your situation   **your situation**   **your situation**

4. I am committed to giving time and money to serve others.

1	2	3	4	5	6	7	8	9	10

Always describes	**Sometimes describes**	**Never describes**
your situation	**your situation**	**your situation**

5. I plan to give to relief organizations that do God's work to help others who will experience a similar financial crisis as I am facing.

1	2	3	4	5	6	7	8	9	10

Always describes	**Sometimes describes**	**Never describes**
your situation	**your situation**	**your situation**

ASSESSING YOUR SCORES

Add up the total value of your scores from each section and enter the number in the chart below:

Income and Money Management	Total: _____
Insurance and Relief Resources	Total: _____
Debts and Obligations	Total: _____
Long-Range Financial Planning	Total: _____
Giving Plan	Total: _____

Grand Total: _____

Your grand total score will fall into one of the three following ranges or zones, giving you immediate feedback on your overall financial wellness.

191–250   Red Zone—Critical Need for Immediate Help

Your financial trauma is at a serious level and you will need immediate professional help. It's never too late to make needed changes, but you will want to get the help of a financial coach to help your progress. We also recommend joining a small group through a church or other faith-based organization in your community that can help and encourage you to formulate a plan. The small group resources later in this book will prove to be crucial for you to improve your situation.

60–190   **Yellow Zone—Take Caution**

It is likely that by making a few changes you can make immediate improvements and drastically improve your situation and lower stress levels. Professional financial coaching may also benefit you. Please see the resources section of this chapter for ideas of tools and resources that may benefit you. We think the small group program will also be of great help.

25–50   **Green Zone—Help Others**

You are doing very well and may be in a situation where you could consider helping others who are facing the same financial crisis you have faced. Clearly you are employing biblical practices for managing money, so you might consider leading a small group or coaching others in your church or community to help them through their crisis. Keep up the good work! We hope you will consider being a small group facilitator and utilize the small group resources in Part III of this book.

SUMMARY

Whether it is a divorce, the loss of a loved one, or a natural disaster you are facing, the impact on your finances is sure to be severe. By taking a thoughtful assessment of your situation, and employing the financial tools and techniques we will introduce in the next chapter, we are certain you can begin to make good progress. It will likely be one of the biggest challenges you will ever face, but remember—there are a lot of people in your community who are facing the same challenges—and there are resources available to help you carry this load. You are not alone in this! By employing the biblical financial principles found in the next chapter, you will be able to rebuild your financial world. Further, by continuing to use the core money management tactics we will share, you will find that they will help you build a strong financial foundation for years to come when life returns to a more even keel.

You have now done the hardest part of the task! You have faced the situation, assessed where you stand, and when you begin the small group sessions in Part III of *Growing through Disaster*, you will gain the support and resources you need to take practical action. Before we move on to the more nuts-and-bolts part of the money management process, here is a helpful checklist for you to use to begin your financial recovery plan:

POST-DISASTER FINANCIAL CHECKLIST

____ Contact insurance companies (property, auto, health/disability [if injured])

____ Contact credit card companies or other lenders about payment plan details

____ Contact employer to discuss support resources and work contingency plans/expectations

____ Apply to FEMA for aid if in a national disaster area

____ Revisit the financial checkup quiz and highlight top areas to address

____ Create your financial organizer to store all your key financial data (three-ring binders or accordion files work well)

Chapter 5

SPENDING PLAN—
MONEY MANAGEMENT
STRATEGIES

*Your way of life should be free from the love of money, and you should be
content with what you have. After all, he has said,
I will never leave you or abandon you.*

—Hebrews 13:5

We must adjust to changing times and still hold to unchanging principles.[1]

—President Jimmy Carter

For many years I (Matt) coached youth basketball, which I'm certain is why
my hair turned grey prematurely! However, despite the fun, stress, and hair-
changing challenges of trying to teach the nuances of the greatest game
ever to kids ages eight to eighteen, one coaching lesson with a parallel to real life
always rang true: you have to have a firm foundation in the fundamentals. Even
with youngsters first learning how to play hoops, when you absolutely had to score
a bucket or stop the other team from scoring at a crucial point in the game, return-
ing to core principles was a key strategy for success. Hustle, strong defense, helping
out your teammate, rebounding, boxing out...doing the little things it takes to win.
These are the foundational qualities it takes to excel on the hardwood. It is no wonder
that John Wooden, famed UCLA basketball coach and man of deep faith in God,
continually extolled these principles to his dominantly successful teams. By looking
to build a firm foundation in the fundamentals, the chance for future success was
greatly increased.

With the type of financial trauma you have faced, you too are at a crucial junc-
ture in the game of life. While your challenge, obviously, is not even remotely com-
parable to putting a ball through a hoop, now more than ever we need to look to

55

bedrock biblical financial principles to help you rebuild your financial world. For twenty-five years I have been teaching five core biblical financial principles to people all over the country. Part of the beauty of this simple approach is that if you are able to live out these five imperatives, it really does not matter where you are in your financial life—high income, low income; rich, poor; young, old; struggling with debt, living with surplus—you will find newfound financial balance and spiritual peace. These five biblical principles are so flexible and all-encompassing that I think you will agree they cover all the core aspects of money management. Even in your time of crisis, these five truths will help lead you back to a place of stability.

FIVE BIBLICAL PRINCIPLES FOR FINANCIAL RECOVERY

The key to the five principles is that they all need to work together to help you recover and achieve biblical financial fitness. Like pistons in an engine, you need all cylinders working smoothly and efficiently to make your financial motor go. If someone is giving 10 percent of their income but also racking up big balances on their credit cards (thinking back to times of "normal" life before the financial trauma), then your financial life is still going to be out of balance. You may be saving some money but not paying much attention to how or where you spend, so you will again be off kilter. The very foundational strength of these five principles is how they mesh together to allow you to build a strong, biblically based financial game plan. Let's explore how they will help your recovery. Our first step may surprise you.

Principle 1: Give Generously (2 Corinthians 9:6-8)

In the book of 2 Corinthians, Paul lays down the main New Testament teaching on giving when he instructs the Christians in Corinth to give generously:

> Remember this: Whoever sows sparingly will also reap sparingly, and whoever sows generously will also reap generously. Each of you should give what you have decided in your heart to give, not reluctantly or under compulsion, for God loves a cheerful giver. And God is able to bless you abundantly, so that in all things at all times, having all that you need, you will abound in every good work. (NIV)

Rather than getting lost in a debate about the law-based tradition of tithing, Paul suggests a new Holy Spirit–driven model of giving based on generosity. Like Paul, I don't want to get bogged down in calculations or an argument of how much you should be giving. If you are in crisis mode, I want to take Paul's lead and focus on the core principle. Giving must come from the heart, no matter the amount. Clayton and I want to be deeply sensitive to the fact you may have lost everything due to the financial trauma you have been through. God knows every nuance of your situation, and he wants to shower you with grace during this difficult time. You very likely may not have anything to give at this point, and that is okay. The Lord understands, and he no doubt wants to provide your base needs and help you get back on track as soon as possible.

However, once your situation stabilizes and you do have some income flowing back in again, we believe it is critically important that your recovery process is fueled by generosity. It may seem counterintuitive to give money away when you may be struggling to get back to normal; however, based on our experience, you can't afford not to honor God first with whatever income he may be providing. When Clayton lost his wife, he gave 10 percent of the life insurance money to God at an uncertain time when he had two little kids to raise on a modest pastor's salary. The $2,000 he donated to his wife's memorial fund was the lead gift in what became $20,000 in loving tribute to a wonderful lady. When Clayton's church started a building project the next year, they learned they were short on funds to complete the planned water feature and baptismal. Remarkably, the cost to finish the baptismal was $20,000, which was what was given to his wife's memorial fund. Every baptism is a tribute to her memory.

> We believe it is critically important that your recovery process is fueled by generosity.

When I lost my job many years back, and the future seemed very dim indeed, my wife and I decided to continue giving generously. She picked up extra shifts at the hospital, and I gave from the small side jobs I found. When I got reestablished and founded my Christian financial training ministry, we actually had more money in our emergency fund than when I lost my job! How could that possibly happen? It made no sense at all, unless you are looking at it from a kingdom perspective—only God can do this sort of stuff!

To be clear, we are not looking at giving 10 percent as some magic formula. Generous giving, as Paul instructed as our guideline, may look very different for your situation. Let God lead your giving as you seek him in prayer. If you are able to give cheerfully, with no guilt, he will show you what generous is for where you are. Regardless, by honoring God with your offering of love during your time of greatest trial, it will lead you to a harvest of spiritual growth and maturity that likely will take you to a point of spiritual breakthrough. In 2 Corinthians 9:10, Paul expands on the generous giving teaching: "Now he who supplies seed to the sower and bread for food will also supply and increase your store of seed and will enlarge the harvest of your righteousness" (NIV).

This may very well be the most important verse in the Bible on giving, and also the most overlooked. Paul takes us to the ultimate payoff, after again reiterating that it is God who provides everything for us, from seed for crops to bread for our basic needs. He does not say that if we give generously, then he will reward us with a Lexus and a Rolex. No! He says that if we give generously, he will enlarge the harvest of our righteousness. By giving with the motive to grow his kingdom, the result will be that we grow in our faith and love for him. So we do, in fact, give to get. But what we get in the end is not more cash and cars; what we get is a deeper relationship with our

Father, more right living (righteousness), and expanded spiritual maturity. Generous giving = deeper faith.

So as you begin to dig out and rebuild, we strongly encourage you to listen first to God on this critically important part of Christian discipleship. No matter where you are in life, times of plenty or times of pain, the temptation is going to be to not give money. The kingdom is vanquished when the devil can convince God's followers that they don't need to give their financial resources back to God's work. For if you don't give, our adversary knows you will also not enlarge the harvest of your righteousness. Even in this time of trial, give what God has led you to give as an act of thankfulness to God and acknowledgment that you will trust him no matter what.

Principle 2: Flee the Love of Money (1 Timothy 6:9-12)

Our second biblical financial principle for financial recovery comes from the book of 1 Timothy, and it is designed to bring us balance and a check against greed and materialism. In the crisis situation you are facing, we could see how it would be very easy to struggle with envy of those who have not lost their life's possessions, or anger at God for having to deal with this financial test. Either way, we must check anger and envy so that they do not become a bitter root in our heart. Further, we do not want to gloss over the real and deep losses you have experienced. This is an exceedingly difficult path to traverse. At a vulnerable time such as this, the evil one is surely taking every opportunity to beat you down and tell you lies about what you have lost. Turning to the strong directive in 1 Timothy 6:9-12 (NIV) may be a guiding light to keep your mind focused on things above:

> Those who want to get rich fall into temptation and a trap and into many foolish and harmful desires that plunge people into ruin and destruction. For the love of money is a root of all kinds of evil. Some people, eager for money, have wandered from the faith and pierced themselves with many griefs. But you, man of God, flee from all this, and pursue righteousness, godliness, faith, love, endurance, and gentleness. Fight the good fight of the faith. Take hold of the eternal life to which you were called when you made your good confession in the presence of many witnesses.

At this point in your life, you may feel as though you should be teaching the class on ruin and destruction! You have experienced the real thing. While Timothy was actually referring to the ruin that can come from falling into the trap of materialism (love of money), these verses have a powerful parallel to one who has been through a physical or personal trauma. It could be easy to wander from your faith right now after being dealt such a severe blow, but Timothy provides a helpful path out of this pit by exhorting us to pursue *righteousness* (there's that word again!), godliness, faith, endurance, love, and gentleness.

The love of money can rear its ugly head in many forms, not just the typical over-focused desire on becoming rich. More subtle expressions of the love of money could simply be hoarding money, envy of what others have, or anxiety and worry about money that causes us to shift our trust away from God to mammon. Remember, money is not the root of all evil; it is the *love* of money. Money is just a tool we can use for good, neutral, or bad purposes. One of the definitions of *love* is: a feeling of warm personal attachment or deep affection, as for a parent, child, or friend.[2] I think it is significant to note, the assumption by definition is that love should be toward another person. If we shift that affection, for whatever reason, including our current state of trauma, to money or possessions, we have corrupted love and its basic human purpose. Timothy was giving us a key life warning: focus our love on the person of God and our family, and then use money as intended as a tool to help us live our lives. His directive is an emphatic command to flee, and ironically, it is not the typical option of fight or flight. It is both fight *and* flight. We should fight the good fight of faith in this time of trial as we endure and trust God instead of money to provide our needs. While at the same time, we are to flee the love of money and the power it has to steal our hearts away from God. So remember, as you work through the challenges of rebuilding your financial world, your response should be not fight *or* flight, but fight *and* flight!

Principle 3: Live Within Your Means (Proverbs 30:7-9)

> Two things I ask of you, LORD; do not refuse me before I die: Keep falsehood and lies far from me; give me neither poverty nor riches, but give me only my daily bread. Otherwise, I may have too much and disown you and say, 'Who is the LORD?' Or I may become poor and steal, and so dishonor the name of my God. (NIV)

Give me only my daily bread. What a great approach to both fleeing the love of money and living out daily life! Living within your means, or making ends meet, is one of the greatest challenges of our time. According to CNBC,[3] credit card debt in the United States topped $1 trillion in 2017, and the average household carried more than $6,300 in unpaid debt on their cards. The added payments, fees, and high interest charges cause stress and undermine sound financial planning. We acknowledge that in the short term as you deal with your particular financial disaster, you may need to rely on a credit card to manage expenses in what could be a very unstable financial landscape. You have to do what you have to do; we get that.

For the long-term, however, we want to help you devise your daily bread plan so that you can begin to make sound and healthy financial progress. In the small group session that follows focused on building your financial recovery plan, a key objective will be to build your monthly recovery spending plan. A main goal will be for you to begin spending less than you bring in each month so you can first begin to cover the costs of your recovery. A mainstay for any financial plan to work, controlling costs and building up savings will be even more critical for one who is in financial recovery mode.

Whenever I taught this concept in my financial seminars, I would frequently ask, "What happens if you spend less money than you make each month and do it for a long time?" There was always an awkward pause of silence. It was not a trick question! Obviously, you wind up saving money. However, it is unfortunately far easier said than done as reflected in the credit card debt stats above. Because you will likely have extra "re-start" costs due to your financial disaster and building your way back to normal life, finding a way to create a savings margin and minimize other nonessential expenses will be paramount.

But please remember this: you will not be in belt-tightening mode forever. Working with families to dig out from debt and overcome financial hardships for decades, I have been surprised with how resistant some people have been to changing their financial habits—even if their financial life is going poorly. I think psychologically, people feel that if they admit they have to give up cable TV, or change their spending habits, or eat out less, they are committing to giving those things up for the rest of their lives. It is as if there is a connection in the mind that says, "If I give up something I desire, then it means I give that up for eternity...or maybe longer!" This could not be farther from the truth of what I want to teach. Obviously, there is nothing inherently wrong with cable, shopping, or eating out if we have a balance in our financial life that does not cause us to go into debt or sacrifice giving to do those things. If we commit to follow all five core biblical principles in this chapter, we can give to God's kingdom work, save money for the future, and enjoy life today. Even if you follow the five principles to a T, I can almost guarantee you will have a non-disaster related financial setback at some point. We all face that. Last year I had the privilege of paying $14,000 to have our basement repaired to alleviate a long-time water issue that we could not solve any other way. Who wants to spend money on that sort of stuff? No one! But it was an "emergency" we could no longer ignore.

> If you plan to live below your means, you will form a biblically based habit that will keep your life in order.

By building a plan during your recovery that ensures you live below your means (e.g., you save money each and every month), you will form a biblically based, financially sound habit that will keep your life in order. Said another way, this will ensure that you are living a life of financial discipleship. In recovery mode, you will need extra money to deal with the unforeseen costs you will face: buying new household items insurance did not cover (clothes, furnishing, or supplies), replenishing your emergency fund if you spent that down, or if you lost your home, restocking your kitchen with all the basics like flour, sugar, condiments, and spices. This may easily cost several hundred dollars depending on your culinary tastes. Just remember, if you have to give some things up, it most likely will be temporary, and if you adopt the wisdom from Proverbs 30, in time you will be back to where you can enjoy a balanced financial life. By committing to living within your means as the top financial principle of your fiscal recovery, you will ensure a sound financial footing as this part of your life begins to heal, as well as forming the foundation for a rock-solid financial future.

As we reflect back on the verses that kicked off this chapter, I find it intriguing that the wisdom writer juxtaposes lies and falsehood with spending too much. There is an inherent falsehood that spending more than we have is going to bring us contentment or a better life. According to the word, there is equal danger in thirst for riches and a poverty mentality, and either state can block us from having the daily relationship of reliance and trust upon the Lord to meet our every material need. As you work to build your recovery plan, we know finding balance will be a challenge, yet financial balance is the very thing that will lead you back to complete fiscal health.

LESSONS FROM THE PAST

As you begin to focus on healing from your crisis and re-building your month-to-month financial plan, here are some sound suggestions to consider:

The proverb says: "For lack of guidance a nation falls, but victory is won through many advisers." Seeking out a qualified and licensed financial advisor to have on your team can often lead to greater financial health and improved strategy. To find a Christian financial advisor in your area, visit: www.kingdomadvisors.com, or seek out a referral from someone you trust.

Make sure you get a good recommendation (especially single moms) from friends or relatives for contractors, car dealers, mechanics, and home repair vendors. It is easy to get taken advantage of in normal times, so be double vigilant when you are vulnerable due to trauma.

Every single trauma victim we spoke with said the same thing: I wish I had had more in cash savings to help deal with the emergency I went through. After paying off debts, first build your emergency fund before any other savings, including retirement. Three to six months of your basic living expenses is recommended as a minimum.

Principle 4: Plan for the Future (Luke 14:28)

Right now you are most likely having a challenging enough time getting to tomorrow, so planning for the future may seem like a completely unreasonable task. Let's look a little deeper. As you continue to recover from your financial disaster, the planning you will want to attempt could very well be "near-future" planning, as opposed to long-range, but it is planning nonetheless. The words of Jesus in Luke 14:28 provide us insight into the importance of planning: "Suppose one of you wants to build a tower. Won't you first sit down and estimate the cost to see if you have enough money to complete it?" (NIV).

Depending on the severity of your financial trauma, you may have a large tower to build indeed. However, remember the Lord is *your* strong tower to help you. To create a "bite-sized chunks" approach to your plan, it might be helpful to start mapping out one- to two-week blocks of time and devising your plans for each segment listed below. Planning is actually just a series of goal-setting sessions and then coming up with the tactics needed to hit those goals. If we break it down to small, simple steps, our hope is it will make the overwhelming task of financial trauma recovery more doable.

Because we will devote an entire chapter to building your financial recovery plan, we are just providing an overview to the importance of the biblical concept of planning at this point. For our summary, Proverbs 16:9 is informative: "In their hearts humans plan their course, but the LORD establishes their steps" (NIV). Planning is an interesting mix of us doing our part to plan our course as best as we are able, but also deferring to the Lord to guide and lead our steps. If we plan our steps with God's motives and purposes in mind, we have countless promises that he will lead us on the narrow path that leads to life.

Principle 5: Use a Spending Plan (Proverbs 27:23-24)

Now for the secret sauce! If you want a game-changing approach to improving your financial situation, look no further than core wisdom found right in the heart of the Bible in the book of Proverbs: "Be sure you know the condition of your flocks, give careful attention to your herds; for riches do not endure forever, and a crown is not secure for all generations" (27:23-24, NIV).

> Having a simple, consistent money management system is the secret to conquering the challenges of personal finance.

Back in the day, sheep and goats were equivalent to our currency today. In ancient times, if something happened to your furry friends, it could result in significant financial hardship. That's why being a shepherd was such a big deal. The wisdom from Proverbs 27 is no less true today; we may just need to contemporize the language a bit. We need to pay careful attention to our money and know the condition of our finances, because by doing so, it has a far-reaching impact on our present lives and the future of our family. As it implies, if we don't pay attention and have some way to order our financial dealings, the funds will not last forever. In fact, it promises that they won't! Riches do not endure forever if we don't manage our money wisely. Worse yet, it could wind up having a negative impact on our kids, our kids' kids, and even our kids' kids' kids! The proverb teaches if we don't have a spending plan today to effectively steward the resources God provides to us, we may wind up hurting our kids and grandkids by passing down a legacy of neglect and the hardships of mismanagement. Who knew something as simple as a monthly money management system could actually change the entire course of your family line? It sounds dramatic, but it really is that important.

I have found in more than twenty-five years of financial ministry, having a simple, consistent money management system is the secret to conquering the challenges of personal finance. Let's face it head on: the challenge you face right now is significant. The reality is that very few people actually follow a spending plan. So now, during this most difficult period, it may be a very opportune time for you to put in place this important biblical principle of using a spending plan.

A true spending plan has two parts, and it is actually fundamentally different than a budget. Calling your monthly money management tool a spending plan instead of a budget is also not just a word game to try to trick you into using a "budget." I avoid that term at all costs due to its negative connotations, inflexibility, and lack of ability to react to the realities of daily living. As we will see, a true spending plan is far more flexible and effective than a traditional budget, because a spending plan involves actively managing the reality of your finances, week to week and month to month, versus a budget that only involves projecting the probability of what might happen with your monthly income and expenses. At the end of the day, if you don't have both parts of a spending plan working for you (more on this coming up), your budget is, in essence, just a bunch of numbers on a piece of paper that may or may not reflect the reality of how you are spending your money. Let's explore a true spending plan.

THE POWER OF A SPENDING PLAN

A spending plan is a flexible, monthly money management tool that guides you to live within your means, pay your bills on time, prioritize your expenses, and plan for the future. As I mentioned previously, a true spending plan also needs to have two parts: the monthly projection and the feedback loop. With the monthly projection you will take a look at your expected income and what you anticipate your expenses will be for the month. In the early stages of recovery, your plan may be quite simple, with your only expenses being food, shelter, and clothing. As rebuilding progresses, other areas of expense will return and you can add them to your plan accordingly. The feedback loop will be the method you choose to live out Proverbs 27:23, how you will pay careful attention to your money. We will explore four options you can choose from to monitor and track your expenses.

Your Recovery Spending Plan

Part 1: Monthly Projection
   Project take-home pay each month
   Estimate what you will spend in each spending category

Part 2: Feedback Loop
   Track your weekly spending
   Compare actual spending to your target for each category
   Adjust and modify plan as needed to live within your means

BUILDING YOUR RECOVERY SPENDING PLAN

We recommend a five-step process for you to follow to set up your financial recovery spending plan. These five steps will hold true for all future spending plans you develop.

Step 1—Determine your monthly take-home pay after all taxes and benefits have been paid.

Step 2—Choose the spending categories you will use for your monthly spending plan (for example: food, clothing, housing, auto, entertainment, and medical/insurance).

Step 3—Allocate the target amount you intend to spend on each category from step 2. Total expenses cannot exceed take home pay from step 1.

Step 4—Track amount you spend each week by category.

Step 5—Adjust, modify, and update plan weekly as needed.

Let's break each step down a bit further to help you identify how to build the most helpful recovery spending plan to lead you back to a firm, faith-based, financial footing. At the end of this section, I will include a sample spending plan so you can get a picture of what steps 1–3 should look like once completed.

Step 1—Determine Monthly Take-Home Pay

Depending on if your financial trauma was due to divorce, a natural disaster, or loss of a spouse, your income plan could vary widely, from working your regular job and "income as normal," to needing short-term government assistance or loans from an employer if your losses are more substantial. Your first step will be to figure out what I call your magic number. You need to get down on paper how much money you will bring home in a month (see sample below and the helpful Spending Plan Worksheet in the small group session on money management). Your magic number will be the total amount of income you bring home per month, after taxes and benefit payments (if any) have been removed. Your magic number is what you will commit to live on for the entire month, and not exceed, so that you follow principle 3 to Live Within Your Means. Remember: there is grace, especially in the first few months after your financial trauma, if you exceed your magic number. However, for long-term health you will need to eventually commit to adjusting your spending to what you are earning. Of special note, if your income fluctuates each month like mine does (Clayton is lucky, he's retired!), you will need to pay even closer attention to steps 3 and 4, as well as building up extra savings for when you have a down month income-wise. Once you have figured out your monthly income number, you will be ready for step 2 of the plan.

Step 2—Expense Categories

Here is where a spending plan can start to become much more flexible than a budget. In step 2, you will want to identify the key areas where you will spend money in the coming month. The Spending Plan Worksheet in the small group session lists eleven categories that I have used for decades in my workshops. I think they capture just about every area in which you might spend money; however, please note that you have the ability to change and update those categories depending on your particular situation. Your spending categories may very well be different than mine, so my spending plan system allows you to build categories or a system that best suits you. For example, my personal spending plan has a dedicated category for gifts (as opposed to lumping gifts in with household/personal items), because gifts always seem to be a bit of a problem area for our family. By altering the categories, or adding temporary categories, we can tailor the plan to our individual needs. I do think over time it can be helpful to have consistent categories so you can compare expenditures year over year to help you craft a strong plan. Let your plan be flexible to identify the right areas where you are spending, and don't be afraid to shift the categories over time as you work and develop your plan to better fit the rhythms of your financial life.

Step 3—Allocate Target Amounts for Each Spending Category

This is a step that for some reason many people skip, so it is another crucial secret for success in my opinion. If you are going to try your hand at archery, but the target you are aiming for is moving down range (or is nonexistent), it is going to be significantly harder to hit the mark, is it not? Therefore, at the beginning of each month, set a target amount you will spend in each of your spending categories. Make sure the total amount you allocate for all categories is equal to or less than your monthly take-home pay (your magic number). Having a target will give you something to aim for and guide your overall spending. It can also help you to prioritize if you should purchase something or not. In steps 4 and 5, you will also see in more detail the importance of entering the monthly target for spending.

However, especially as you are working through recovery, you may find that the amounts you spend in each area are changing quite a bit month to month. If you were the victim of a flood or fire, for example, you may spend a lot on clothes or food the first couple of recovery months as you rebuild. I do spend a few minutes each month thinking through what I will need to spend in each category for the coming month as part of the planning process (remember principle 4: Plan for the Future). We have four birthdays in February in our family, so I need to allocate more to gifts than normal and adjust my plan accordingly. So hopefully you can see the value behind this simple step and invest a few minutes to determine what spending areas you may need to focus on for the coming month. Regardless, the most important concept is for your total spending to be less than your total income so you will start saving.

Step 4—Track Your Expenses

Now the proverbial rubber is really going to meet the road. In steps 1–3 above, we completed Part 1 of a monthly spending plan, the projection, where we examined both possible income and probable monthly expenses. With steps 4 and 5, we begin to build Part 2 of your plan, the feedback loop, which includes the process of figuring out where in the world all that money is going every month! Very few people follow Proverbs 27 and track where their money is spent; however, as you work to rebuild your financial life, I would suggest this step is more crucial than any other. If income is particularly scarce, making sure every dollar counts and is spent to meet your basic needs is vital. Wasted dollars at this phase will hurt four times worse than during normal life. Tracking spending will be a lifeline.

> ## Most good things in life involve work!

Like most of the good things that come in life, this step involves some work. We all work hard for the money we earn; should we not work just as diligently in how we spend it? Based on my financial coaching experience, you will find that once you get the rhythm of expense tracking and establish your personal system, tracking expenses will seem like a warm winter coat and wool socks. Maybe not the most glamourous part of your wardrobe, but they are essential for keeping us warm, dry, and protected from the elements. The benefits of tracking where your money is going are noteworthy, especially as you rebuild your financial life,

- It makes you feel as though you are ahead rather than behind in your money dealings.
- Knowing where you spend virtually guarantees you will not spend too much money.
- Tracking helps you avoid wasted dollars.
- It provides helpful information so you make informed spending decisions.
- Tracking expenses helps you better prioritize where you spend.

There are four basic ways you can order your spending plan. Each approach has pros and cons; therefore, my goal is to help you find which system works best for *you*. I actually follow a hybrid system where I combine elements from the written and electronic styles. This is the goal, to build your personalized tracking system. My approach is not "My way or the highway." I prefer "Your way for progress today." Money is emotional and personal. My system for managing money may not work for you, but you have to have some system that adheres to the five biblical principles we explored. I trust that you know what will work best for you. Then you can tweak your plan so that it is easy for you to use, fits your style, is repeatable each month, and provides you the benefits listed above. The chart below describes each option for how you might track expenses each week or month. With more and more of our financial transactions becoming electronic, most people will find they may use a hybrid of the options.

Expense Tracking Options

SYSTEM	PROS	CONS
MENTAL Tracking of expenses Rely on memory and estimation to meet obligations and manage discretionary funds	No software or apps to learn Less paperwork Simple May require less time	Easy to overlook key bills and automatic debit transactions; Hard to see the big picture of financial situation. No visual representation of your plan No long-term records to see patterns Less accurate, relies on bank debit records, and won't catch institutional errors Less effective for tax record purposes
CASH ONLY Tracking of expenses Rely on cash-envelope category system to modify behavior in problem discretionary spending areas.	Can work well if person has great self control. Can help you focus on problem spending areas	Security issues of keeping cash on hand No interest earned on cash balances Time consuming to manually pay bills using cash, requiring payment in person, transportation, etc. Less efficient: Online bill pay or autopayment isn't utilized No long term records to view behavior or spending patterns

SYSTEM	PROS	CONS
WRITTEN Tracking of expenses Use a written ledger to track expenses and plan monthly income and expenses.	Provides immediate visual overview of expenses in form of a ledger or spreadsheet Simple and effective. Easy to compare spending between categories. Strong for record keeping. Can be used to track any type of transaction, includ-ing electronic or autopay options	Does not interface with online banking or invest-ment info. Ledger may seem intimidat-ing to some.
ELECTRONIC Tracking of expenses Use software or phone app to record all expenses	Efficient; easier to balance bank account, download data, run reports, and build financial history.	Requires access to wi-fi/internet and electronic devices Can be time consuming. Risk of data loss, corruption, hacking. Not effective if you don't run reports.

Step 5—Adjust and Modify

A spending plan is different and superior to a budget. A spending plan allows your monthly plan to be flexible, interactive, and adjustable. Mid-month modifying of the plan allows you to make the kinds of changes that are required to deal with real life. Take time each week to add up the total amount you have spent in each category and com-pare this figure with your monthly spending targets. This ensures you are within your goal and not overspending. However, if you find you have overspent in a category, or are at risk to do so, don't stress. It's not too late. Because you are checking in mid-month, you still have time to adjust spending up or down in other areas. Do you see the beauty of the flexibility here? And it does not take that much time to quickly add this all up. I also add up my total expenses each week and compare this sum with what income I've earned so far for the month as another mid-month gauge. If you are not doing these weekly subtotals and comparisons to targets, you will be flying blind and unsure of where you stand.

CREDIT CARDS AND FINANCIAL RECOVERY

If you have access to a credit card, and most people do, you will want to form a careful strategy for card use during your recovery phase. Realistically, your situation may be dire and access to other funds limited or nonexistent. While I am a big proponent of only using credit cards if you pay them off each month, I also realize that you may temporarily need to use a card to handle expenses from your financial emergency. Here are some helpful guidelines to follow so that you do not fall into a credit trap. Before tapping a credit card, fully explore all other options:

- Emergency funds/savings

- Obtain resources available from relief organizations, churches, or nonprofits

- Borrow funds from a friend or family member if possible

Contact the card company and fully explain your financial crisis situation. (I suggest you only speak with a manager, and get whatever is agreed upon in writing). If you are in a nationally declared disaster area, see if the card company will waive late fees and interest charges for a certain amount of time. If needed, inquire about the option of an increase in your credit limit, even if temporary. I would also see if they will lower your base interest rate. Set a maximum limit of the amount you plan to borrow using credit cards.

In the best-case scenario, before accessing credit, map out your plan for how you will reduce your debt once you are in a better position. Realistically, your recovery could take three to five years. It would be understandable to overspend your income by 10–30 percent in year one depending on your disaster. If you access credit for your recovery, be sure to plan to live on only 80 percent of your income in subsequent years so that you can pay down debt.

SAMPLE MONTHLY RECOVERY SPENDING PLAN

If you have never built a spending plan before, it does not need to be an overly complicated exercise, and it will take less time than you might think. While you will need to tailor your plan to your specific situation, the sample plan will give you a template for what you will need to build your recovery spending plan. In the sample below, we are assuming expenses for a family of four, three months after a tornado hit their home. They are now in an apartment waiting for the insurance company to complete their claim and FEMA to clear debris from their neighborhood so that they can begin to rebuild their home. You will have a chance to build your recovery spending plan in the small group session that accompanies this chapter.

SAMPLE RECOVERY
SPENDING PLAN

Income

Income after taxes/benefits:	$3,750

Expenses

Giving	$160
Housing/Utilities	$1,400
Food	$550
Clothing	$200
Transportation	$200
Medical/Insurance	$300
Household/Personal	$200
Entertainment	$140
Professional Expense	$0
Saving/Investment	$300
Debts	$250
Other: Gifts	$50
Other: _____	$ _____

Total Expenses	**$3,750**

SUMMARY: PRINCIPLES TO LIVE BY

As you embark on building your financial recovery plan, these five biblical principles—give generously, flee the love of money, live within your means, plan for the future, and use a spending plan—will form a solid, balanced approach to managing your money God's way. The spending plan should be the key tool to guide your day-to-day money management so that you can get back on your feet. It will provide you vital information to ensure you cover all your bills and begin to plan for post-recovery living. The small group sessions in *Growing through Disaster* will take us to the next step and allow you to delve into the practical and establish more specific financial recovery plans. Continue to seek God's word for key strategies to managing the money he provides.

Chapter 6

PLANNING—
YOUR FINANCIAL
RECOVERY PLAN

Dishonest money dwindles away,
but whoever gathers money little by little makes it grow.
—Proverbs 13:11, NIV

How we handle our money is of great concern to God because it
indicates what's really important to us. If our goal is to put ourselves first
and provide just for our comfort and security, then that's how we'll spend our
money. But if God is at the center of our lives,
we'll want to use our money for His Glory.
—Billy Graham

At this crucial time in your life, you may feel as though you need something extra to help you cope and deal with the challenge you are facing. Day in, day out, year over year, it never ceases to amaze me how the Bible can be that constant source of inspiration, the healing balm to every wound, care, and concern. Even a simple and basic function like planning does not escape the Lord's eye and takes on new power and meaning when filtered through the Spirit: "The LORD's spirit will rest upon him, a spirit of wisdom and understanding, *a spirit of planning* and strength, a spirit of knowledge and fear of the LORD" (Isa 11:2, emphasis added).

Did you catch that? A Holy Spirit–inspired sense of planning. Who knew planning could be so spiritual? It may seem strange to consider, but the Holy Spirit can endow us with enhanced spiritual ability to plan. I also like that in the verse, planning and strength are placed side by side, inferring that sound planning precedes and leads to strength. Planning in this context is a core component of the character that will come from the root of Jesse, King David's father and the spiritual lineage of the messiah. We pray God will give you an increased ability to plan and added strength to make it through this challenging time. To me, planning is another way of trying to protect my family and show them the love of God by taking care of them as best I can.

As you recover, you will likely need to engage in future planning in the following areas. You may not have issues in each area, so skip any categories where you feel you have things covered:

Food acquisition

Clothing

Housing arrangements

Transportation options

Monthly cash flow

Dealing with your job

Dealing with insurance or legal matters

I would suggest mapping out in written form recovery goals in each category where you have need for the next week, month, and one- to three-month time periods (so you can refer back to your goals and check completed goals off as you accomplish tasks). If needed, or when you are ready, you can then add planning for longer-term goals like one- to three-year and three- to five-year time frames. But first things first; let's focus on the here and now. In the first financial small group session in this book, we provide a basic and simple planning exercise to start you thinking about how to break down recovery into small, manageable steps. In the third small group session, we will help you expand on your beginning steps and broaden your personal recovery plan as noted above. For now, refer to the chart below to visualize a potential longer-range goal plan.

By mapping out some basic goals and developing the steps needed to reach each goal, you will begin to feel that you are making progress. Proverbs 21:5 provides us with a beacon of truth about planning: "The plans of the diligent end up in profit, but those who hurry end up with loss." This verse infers that failing to plan will lead to loss. Working on specific plans will be profitable to help you combat possible feelings of helplessness or frustration from your circumstances. We don't have all the answers for your unique situation, but we do feel that the wisdom of scripture can guide us to begin taking the steps needed to move forward with God's help by engaging in some basic life and financial planning.

FINANCIAL RECOVERY PLAN

In this sample plan, we are assuming the family is in temporary housing due to a flood (non-national disaster area). Their car was totaled, and they are trying to get back to their workplace, which was not damaged.

NEXT WEEK'S PLAN

Objective	Goal	Finish-by Date	Check-off Box
Auto	Call insurance co. Get rental car	Mon., June 1	
Work	Call boss/set plan	Mon., June 1	
Food	Visit food bank	Tues., June 2	
Clothing	Call friends	Tues., June 2	
Financial	Call credit card co.	Wed., June 3	

NEXT MONTH'S PLAN

Objective	Goal	Finish-by Date	Check-off Box
Cash Flow	Begin tracking expenses	Ongoing	
Auto	Replace car	Once insurance $ received	
Insurance	Settle homeowner's claim	July 1	

THREE MONTH PLAN

Objective	Goal	Finish-by Date	Check-off Box
Financial	Rebuild ER fund monthly $200 to savings account	Aug. 15	
Housing	Begin cleanup when safe	Aug. 25 (tentative)	
Clothing	Replace basic wardrobe, $700	Aug. 31	

Here is another helpful list for you to review from the Consumer Financial Protection Bureau.[1] Consider referring back to this list when you work on your specific long-range plan in the final small group section of this book. Incorporate any of the needed steps into your personal plan.

As soon as possible:

- If your home, car, or property was damaged by the storm, contact your insurance company to start the claims process.

- Ask for a copy of your insurance policy if you don't have one available. It will help you verify your coverage.

- Damage to your home does not nullify your responsibility to pay your mortgage. However, many mortgage servicers have been told they can help homeowners affected by the storm. So you should contact your mortgage servicer and tell them about your situation.

- If you don't have a monthly mortgage statement or coupon book with you, search the Mortgage Electronic Registration Systems (MERS) or call them toll-free at (888) 679-6377 to find the company that services your mortgage.

- Take a look at your income and savings and determine how much money you have available to pay bills and creditors.

- If your income is interrupted and you don't think you will be able to pay your credit cards or other loans, be sure to contact your lenders as soon as possible. Explain your situation and when you think you will be able to resume normal payments. The important thing is to make the calls before your next payments are due.

- If you are in a presidentially declared disaster area, you may qualify for disaster assistance. Check with the Federal Emergency Management Agency (FEMA) for more information.

- If your home is damaged to the point that you can't live in it, contact your utility companies and ask to suspend your service. This could help free up money in your budget for other expenses.

- Take a look at your bills and set priorities. Your mortgage, rent, and insurance payments should stay high on your list.

As you rebuild:

- Be careful if you choose to hire a public adjuster to help with your insurance claim. Be sure the adjuster is licensed to do business in your state. Also, watch out for red flags such as big upfront fees, requests for a suspicious amount of personal information, referrals to contractors of their preference only, and false or inflated claims. Don't pay a large sum up front before you know if the adjuster is going to help you. Many states put a limit on fees. False claims are fraud against the insurance company. (Some con artists may pose as adjusters to steal your personal information.)

- Get bids from several local, established contractors. And avoid contractors who who sell door-to-door, are from out of state, and who do not provide a physical address and phone number, or refuse to show identification.

- Ask if the contractor has the required licensure, and request and verify license numbers. Check with your state licensing agency's website or hotline to make sure the licenses are valid. Ask the licensing agencies if the contractor has a history of complaints.

When working with contractors, we suggest keeping these cautions in mind:

- Never pay in advance.

- Never pay in cash.

- Never sign anything before carefully reading it.

- Never provide personal financial information such as your checking account number or debit/credit card number.

- If you have to borrow funds to pay for repairs, avoid letting the contractor steer you toward a particular lender.

YOUR GRAB AND GO EMERGENCY KIT

My (Matt's) wonderful mentor, John Gilman, was always fond of saying, "Now is the time for love." It was advice that could never be wrong. When viewed in the context of planning, I followed John's lead and coined my own catchphrase: *Planning is love in advance.* Building your grab and go emergency kit will help you prepare for the next emergency and shows love for your family.

A grab and go emergency kit is an essential planning element. This kit will take time to build, but it includes basic survival supplies as well as critical financial and legal information you need in the face of an emergency. We realize that if you are currently in the midst of a crisis that has impacted your shelter, livelihood, and property, building an emergency kit may seem too late. However, while displaced or entering into a recovery phase, it can be more important than ever to get organized and keep important resources and documents together. With other financial traumas beyond natural disasters such as divorce, loss of a loved one, or loss of income, you would benefit from building an emergency preparedness kit.

We recommend scanning copies of important documents and saving a backup of these items for ease of access: the "cloud" (such as Google drive) if you are confident with housing your personal data online; on a jump drive or CD; and as hard copies secured in a waterproof storage container. (A CD, while bulkier, may hold up better to the elements. Since they are inexpensive, easy to obtain, and lightweight, you may want to include both a CD and a jump drive, for backup purposes, in your kit.)

Make sure your grab and go emergency kit is easily accessible, portable, and secure. Based on the type of disaster you face, lack of access to power, computers, or the internet could impede access to the data you need in your kit. If you use the cloud, keep in mind that public libraries have computers available for public use. Further, from a data security standpoint, you may not be comfortable storing personal data in the cloud. No storage device is one hundred percent impervious to theft, cyber or physical, and experts vary on if you should store this type of data in the cloud. While it may seem old-fashioned, a hard copy may be most reliable if faced with a natural disaster.

> In the same way, faith is dead when it doesn't result in faithful activity.
>
> —James 2:17

In addition to compiling important papers and financial documents, we recommend also having other essential items on hand such as nonperishable food, clean (bottled) water, prescription and over-the-counter medicines, first aid items, and extra cell phone chargers. (Note: Dry-pack camping meals are great for your emergency kit because they are lightweight and are surprisingly tasty.)

COLLECTING PERSONAL RECORDS

Below is a list of the personal records you would want to have saved to your grab and go emergency kit electronic file storage system, though an organized file of paper copies should also be stored as a backup. Many find it helpful to use an accordion file folder to place any hard copies of documents along with physical items such as a book of checks, cash, and your file storage device. It is compact and easy to grab if you have time based on your emergency situation.

___ Photographs of every family member

___ Photographs of other loved ones you may need (parents, grandparents)

___ Military records

___ Medical and immunization records

___ Marriage license and/or divorce decree

___ Grade reports/transcripts for children for each placement

___ Special-needs documentation

__ Resume and copy of college transcripts

__ Will, trust, powers of attorney, and medical directives

__ Financial documents

__ Front page of all insurance policies or annuity contracts

__ Recent property tax bill

__ Recent copy of bank statement

__ Copy of credit report

__ List of investments and account numbers

__ A book of checks for your checking account

__ Car titles

__ Mortgage deed with account number or rental lease agreement

---

LESSONS FROM THE PAST

Mark hits a financial crisis in chapter 12 when he loses his job. We have listed some lessons Mark and others have learned to aid the path of recovery:

Patience is key. Do not be surprised if it takes you anywhere from two to five years to recover from your financial trauma.

Fear and uncertainty are common tools of the evil one to trip you up. Women more so than men lose jobs due to divorce because of the emotional strain or need to care for the kids, so trusting God in the process is critical to maintaining overall health.

Everyone should have an emergency box like the grab and go emergency kit highlighted in this chapter. Be sure to have three to four days' worth of food, water, medical supplies, and survival gear. Don't forget your medications, diapers, and baby formula (if needed).

Make sure you have your eye on the ball. If married, often one spouse will turn all financial matters over to the other because he or she is better at fiscal management. Even if you are not the person paying the bills, it is important to know what is going on with your finances.

LEGACY PLANNING—ADDRESSING ESTATE ISSUES WITH LOVE

The old saying about the only certainties in life being death and taxes, while true, may miss the core emotional veracity of the maxim. What is perhaps more certain is that people really just want to ignore death and taxes, as well as their boring cousin, estate planning! Why is something that is so important so confusing and tedious?

The reality is right now you probably have enough on your plate with the emotional and financial trauma you have been working through. No doubt it has been hard enough. Why would you even want to think about death and taxes too? Truly nothing in life is easier to ignore and avoid than estate planning. You probably just fell asleep at my very mention of the topic! Despite this fact, estate planning is a crucial component of wise financial planning. Now that you have had a traumatic life event, perhaps one that was even life threatening, it is actually timely to address a few key planning issues. Money management is so important and all-reaching, it may be the only thing we still have to do after we die!

My pastor (Matt) at our church in Kansas City, Jon Bowles, is a master at taking a topic and spinning it around to look at it from a new and unexpected angle, uncovering a spiritual revelation in the process. It is a rare gift in teaching. I am going to attempt to spin estate planning in a similar manner in hopes we can glean a new nugget of truth. If we switch our focus from estate planning (boring!) to "leaving a legacy of love" (much better!), I think it will help you embrace an important planning activity. Who does not want to be loving and leave a positive and lasting legacy? Those sound like two things we would all want to do.

> Do the loving thing with your money.

"So what exactly are you trying to trick me into doing here, Matt?" you may ask. The truth of the matter is you really don't have to do anything if you don't want to. You already have an estate plan, and you may have not even known it. Plus it is 100 percent free of charge. Now, that does not mean it is a *good* plan, the *best* plan, or the plan *you* want.

Regrettably, the no-cost, no-work plan is also the one that is provided by the government, or more accurately, by the state where you currently reside (for US citizens). The state you live in definitely has a plan for what will happen to your assets and property when you pass away. However, the state's plan may not even be close to the plan you would want for the distribution of your possessions, and that is why this topic is so crucial. The state's plan may not reflect your wishes to support ministry, and it may very well cost your estate a boatload of money. Good stewardship (a.k.a., financial discipleship) extends to making sure we have a plan for how the resources God gave us during this life are passed on so that they continue to bless others and build his kingdom after we are gone. Planning now will lead to love later.

At its most simple level, what I prefer to call "legacy of love planning" is making sure you have a will or trust in place (and a couple of other important legal documents) to direct what happens to your stuff after you shed the mortal coil. Another way of saying this is that you are going to do the loving thing with your money—ensuring that you show love to your family and God by having a plan in place for both now and the end of life on this planet. Seeing the uncertainty of life as you have just witnessed firsthand, you may be highly motivated to accomplish this task. If you work with a qualified estate planning lawyer, he or she will do most of the heavy lifting for you. Creating your legacy of love plan may even be easier than you think and far less costly than not setting it up. If you work at a large company, you may even have a prepaid legal benefit program that can make setting all this up much easier. Failing to have a legacy of love plan almost always leads to family strife, costly legal work, unwanted surprises, and headaches.

YOUR LEGACY OF LOVE PLAN

When it comes to legacy planning, generally speaking you can create a "pay a little bit now but pay a lot more later" plan, or you can set up a "pay a bit more now and pay next to nothing later" plan. It depends on your situation, of course, how you want to distribute your assets, and your overall net worth. This is where a good lawyer can really help you decide what is right for you and help you chart your course.

Going a bit deeper, Option 1 (less cost now, likely more later) is having a will prepared, which may cost approximately $250–$500. A will costs less than a trust; however, it offers less control, less privacy, and less options; and it may cost your heirs a lot of money in probate and legal fees after you go to heaven. Probate process costs can often run from $2,500 to $25,000 or more, depending on your estate. Option 2 is to create a trust that may carry an initial price tag of $1,500 to $3,000 on average, but when you pass away, your heirs have virtually no additional court or legal expenses. The accompanying chart gives a comparison of using a will versus a trust. One very important point to note: when you enlist a lawyer to create a trust for you, you will also get a will in the package (and your lawyer will explain how they work together).

A legal will is critically important if you have minor children or any dependents. In the will you can name who you want to raise your children and serve as legal guardian should something happen to you. Otherwise, a judge is going to determine who raises your child or children if no will is on file, and he or she may choose a family member you would not have selected. This alone is the most important reason to have a legacy of love plan. Our kids are our most prized "possession," for lack of a better term, and the will ensures they are placed in the hands we choose. What could be more traumatic for your child, after losing his or her parents, to have to be raised by someone who was not selected by mom or dad?

Legacy of Love Plan Options[2]

	Will	Trust
Cost to set up *Individual* (Will only) *Couple**	 $200-500 $500 - $1,000	 $1,500-$3,000 $2,000 -$3,500^
Subject to probate Probate cost Managed distribution options Public record Helps if incapacitated Changeable	Yes $2,500-$25,000+ No Yes No Yes	No $0 Yes No Yes Yes

* Price would include creation of all other important planning documents referenced later in this chapter.

^ All costs listed for trusts would include a will and the other important planning documents referenced later in this chapter.

The most common advantage of a trust over a will, aside from long-term costs, is the concept of managed distribution. When you pass away, your assets have to be distributed to someone. If you have only a will, the distribution is accomplished through a one-time delivery of assets and property to the beneficiary or beneficiaries. Once approved by the probate process (which is a court process open to the public), the transfer of all assets occurs, the process is done, and all assets must be distributed immediately. That can be an issue depending on the age, financial expertise, and maturity of your heirs.

A trust gives you more flexibility, control and privacy.

If you have a trust created, the distribution of assets is private and can occur immediately, or over the course of months and even years. Because the trust owns the assets, not the deceased, the successor trustee, whom you appoint, would disburse funds at the direction of the deceased and the rules of the trust. This gives the deceased a lot more control, flexibility, and options for distribution. For example, if a parent dies young, they may not want a nineteen-year-old to inherit a sizable amount of money before he or she is able to handle it. The trust ensures that the basic needs of that nineteen-year-old are met, and it also allows for the wishes of the deceased to be met in terms of how the money is used. You cannot accomplish delayed disbursement options with a will. In my personal trust, our kids cannot get any funds aside from basic health and maintenance needs until they are twenty-two. From twenty-two to thirty-six, they can only request to receive money from the trust that is equal to what they personally earned for the year, as proven on their IRS Form W-2. This ensures that they have to work to receive benefit from the trust until they are older and hopefully more established and equipped to manage what they might inherit. With a trust, as you can see from this example, you can be much more creative with how your assets are passed on. By the way, if my kids want to take a year off from age eighteen to twenty-four and embark on a year-long mission trip or ministry assignment, the trustee of the trust can also approve funds to cover that wish. Either way, I am able to continue helping my kids be responsible or support kingdom work after I'm gone.

PROTECT YOUR FAMILY

In addition to a will or trust, there are several other key legal documents you will want to have in place to help protect your family. Having these documents allows you to do the loving thing for your family by making decisions ahead of time like health-care decisions, and end-of-life decisions. I know…not the most fun topics, but having these documents will alleviate a lot of stress on your loved ones. That's a decision you will be glad you made. Your lawyer will be able to help you create each of the key documents. The following chart gives a breakdown of each of the important planning documents.

IMPORTANT LEGAL DOCUMENTS TO PROTECT YOUR FAMILY

Will: a written document that directs how your assets are to be distributed upon your passing.

Trust: a legal entity that you transfer your assets to, and then you control as trustee while you are living. Upon death, the trust document contains provisions for how your assets are to be distributed. Distribution could be immediate or over the course of many years.

Living will: also called a medical directive or advanced directive. This legal document allows a person to specify what actions should be taken if they are in an end-of-life situation and are no longer able to make decisions for themselves because of illness or incapacity.

Power of attorney for health care: allows another person to act on your behalf for health decisions if you are temporarily incapacitated.

Power of attorney for finances: allows another person to act on your behalf for financial decisions if you are temporarily incapacitated.

Life insurance / long-term care insurance: insurance policies that provide money to your loved ones if you die, or they provide benefits if you get sick and need long-term care services.

Inventory of assets: a list of all your bank, brokerage, investment, and retirement accounts, with account numbers. Physical property and all other valuables should also be included. This list helps your loved ones upon your passing so that it is easy to notify the appropriate parties regarding retitling or renaming assets.

Due to the complex nature of legacy planning, Clayton and I strongly suggest you obtain the services of a professional to help you create your legacy of love plan.

LOOKING AHEAD—FULLY RECOVERED

Looking to the future, you will at some point want to develop a longer-range financial plan. Culture is changing so rapidly now that five- to ten-year plans are a bit archaic, but setting long-range goals is always a good exercise if you hold to enough flexibility that you can adjust as needed. It is not out of the question that recovery from a divorce, loss of spouse, or a natural disaster could take three to five years to get back to your new normal. Take your time and take small steps, but always remember to celebrate your successes. Proverbs 13:11 provides timeless wisdom when it comes to planning: "Dishonest money dwindles away, but whoever gathers money little by little makes it grow" (NIV). Fast financial fixes and get-rich-quick philosophy rarely, if ever, leads to God's best. Often they are counter to the Lord's biblical wisdom. If you follow the proverb to gather and restore little by little, scripture promises that following the "get rich slow" plan in Proverbs 13 will lead to growth. When the time is right, expand your plan with a longer time horizon to fit your situation following the principles you have learned here.

PART III

SIX SMALL GROUP
STUDIES

God, grant me the serenity to accept the things I cannot change;
the courage to change the things I can;
and the wisdom to know the difference.
—attributed to Reinhold Niebuhr

Each of the next six chapters provides an opportunity for recovery group participants to take a deeper dive into the relief, recovery, and restoration phases of disaster care. Chapters 7, 8, and 9 will amplify and offer applications for the personal and spiritual trauma healing materials introduced in chapters 1, 2, and 3. Chapters 10, 11, and 12 will provide stewardship-based financial application tools for the recovery strategies presented in chapters 4, 5, and 6. Appendix B provides guidelines for the pastor/facilitator(s) to use in leading the six small group studies.

The goal for the first three recovery group sessions is to create a safe place where trauma victims can express themselves honestly, find hope, and prayerfully seek to grow. The confidential setting of the group allows for the sharing of doubts and beliefs. Thoughts, feeling, and questions can be expressed in a way that helps each participant. Biblically based study, stories, testimonies, and genuine discussion will generate care, healing, and a common concern that God will bless. The result is faith will grow. You may observe participants grow closer to each other and God through these six session studies. Additionally, the closing healing service is an opportunity to celebrate your progress and success.

It is recommended that each of the next six chapters utilize the following small group study agenda as guided by the pastor/facilitator(s):

Opening prayer

Welcome and introductions

Icebreaker questions

Review of chapter synopsis

Key discussion questions

Sharing words of encouragement

Scripture study and discussion

Review of practical applications and take-a-ways

Closing summary of the group study, including joys and concerns

Review of tools and resources

Closing prayer

Chapter 7 speaks to the victim and volunteer. The quality of care and best practices are described. Emotional and spiritual healing of trauma wounds is vitally important to build a resilient faith. A pastor's disaster recovery story from Hurricane Katrina is informative and inspirational.

Chapter 8 describes the five tasks for healing disaster-related trauma. Participants are encouraged to write their recovery plan. An anonymous story of a man who was suicidal tells his story of faith and restoration. Other helpful lessons include a Bible study discussion, life applications, and action steps to help you move forward on your road to recovery.

Chapter 9 sparks the reigniting of hope that comes through God's love. Bruce Blumer writes about his experience and reflections on serving on a Hurricane Harvey disaster recovery team. He begins by asking, "Why serve?" The answers are poignant and encouraging. This chapter identifies many biblically based attributes of God's love that we often take for granted. In our time of need, God's love, mercy, and grace are our lifeline to hope.

As we turn to the final three small group studies, chapter 10 will aid you in taking a practical assessment of your financial situation and help you hone in on which financial areas need your greatest attention. You will begin to set some simple recovery goals, and vignettes in each small group session will provide insight and inspiration for your recovery.

In chapter 11, you will utilize the five biblical principles for financial recovery to begin building your personal monthly spending plan. A worksheet is provided to help you craft your personal plan. Emphasis will be placed on tracking your expenses and strategies to help you live within your means.

In our final small group session, chapter 12 will focus on more extensive planning exercises to form your immediate, monthly, and intermediate-term recovery plans. Use the motivation to build a basic plan to also construct your legacy of love plan for the future (estate plan).

Chapter 7

VICTIM AND VOLUNTEER— CARING MATTERS

Everything that came from Jesus' lips worked like a magnifying glass to focus human awareness on the two most important facts of life: God's overwhelming love for humanity, and the needs for people to accept that love and let it flow through them.

—Huston Smith

Group Study 1

Welcome and Introductions

Opening Prayer (spoken in unison)

> *Gracious God, we come to you as we seek the light of the dawning of a new day after the storm-filled night. Give us light and help us see you. When disaster numbs our souls, let the light of your love warm our hearts. When our doubts assail us, give us stronger faith. When we start to lose our way, guide us. Grant us a new vision for a better tomorrow. Bless us, Lord, with your presence and purpose as we follow the light of Christ. Amen.*

Icebreaker Question: How did you find out about our group and why are you here?

SYNOPSIS OF CHAPTER 1: RELIEF—HOW THE CHURCH CAN HELP?

Clayton tells his Volunteers in Mission (VIM) story of offering relief to the people of Honduras after Hurricane Mitch. He stresses the importance of supporting local pastors and leaders to provide what is really most needed. Faith communities offer social ties and connections that are essential for recovery. Understanding trauma is another essential for helping others who need healing. Scripture has offered comfort and assurance to people of faith dealing with disasters for thousands of years. Resilience is an ability to withstand and recover from a disaster. Our collaboration with the local church can be essential in providing relief and recovery resources. Volunteers in mission projects are beneficial and essential.

Key Discussion Questions

1. Why is it important to provide support to the local community and church leaders?

2. How can your faith community better serve and help others?

3. How has the trauma of disaster impacted you and others you know?

4. Who and what has been most helpful to you in disaster recovery? Why?

  LESSONS FROM THE PAST

I first met Pastor Rod on a Hurricane Katrina relief project in 2006. Our project team visited his local church. Our church leadership was so impressed with Pastor Rod's leadership and the community outreach of his congregation that we offered our support. There is much to learn from Rod's story of relief, recovery, and restoration.

I asked Pastor Rod these questions:

How can a disaster relief team better help a local church after a disaster?

- Realize that the pastors are busy and buried in the needs of their family and church family.

- Help pastors communicate first with the victims and then coordinate volunteers.

- The good intentions of the volunteers are appreciated, but volunteers need to first focus on the priorities of the pastor, the Federal Emergency Management Administration (FEMA), and other community leaders.

- Because of the lack of communication, much patience is required.

- Most pastors will say to the volunteers, "Go hug my people first, listen to them, pray with them, and hold their hand. Help them if you can."

- Ask the victims, "What do you need?" Invite them to tell their story.

- Realize early decisions about recovery plans are difficult. Patience is required.

- Volunteers can be one part of the problem without good coordination and clear communication.

What lessons did you learn in the first few years of recovery?

- The victims are devastated, brokenhearted, and overwhelmed.

- Pain and suffering brings out greater compassion for most victims.

- Most people help each other with great intentions.

- For some, disasters cause greater greed, looting, and stealing.

- The spirit of generosity is amazing, especially from churches across the nation.

- Advocate for the needs of your community.

- Collaboration is critical.

What were some of the most important things that you and your church leaders decided immediately?

- To hold weekly worship (without resources) in our parking lot and then at a temporary location. I managed to lead worship with only a Bible. Every week I offered hope. I did not miss a Sunday for sixty Sundays in a row.

- Our church put the needs of our members and nearby community members first. We waited to rebuild our church building. We decided not to relocate but to rebuild at the same location.

- I realized that I had to make the needs of my family a priority. I also had to practice self-care so that I would not develop severe compassion fatigue.

- We decided that we would help anyone and everyone who needed help.

- We also held a weekly potluck meal and prayer service that helped bond us together as a church family—rich and poor alike.

- I continued being part of a clergy small group that met weekly. We supported and consulted with each other. Meeting with my peers and other pastors on a regular basis was unbelievably helpful to me for many years.

How would you describe the impact of trauma in the months and years following Katrina?

- People need both immediate and long-term tender love and care.

- After a while we don't want to hear the "K" word.

- Some people cannot handle the intensity of the trauma and are quick to relocate.

- We become survivors together. We understand each other.

- We are all in this together no matter our social, economic, or racial background.

- The spirit of giving and receiving is healing for all of us.

- Our personal faith grew especially in ways that healed our hurts and trauma.

- When everything was gone, almost everyone found God.

- Listening and small groups were vital to healing and hope.

- God's grace was evident as we all felt like we were naked before the Lord.

- Social ties in our church are essential for our trauma healing.

- Gratitude to God matters most.

- We want to express gratitude to agencies like the United Methodist Committee on Relief, church volunteers, our bishop and conference staff, many other United Methodist churches, Federal Emergency Management Administration, and others.

Group Discussion Questions:

1. Why are family, church family, and social ties so important for trauma healing?

2. What parts of a worship service really speak to you, and why?

3. What part of the interview with Pastor Rod spoke to you and why?

WORDS OF ENCOURAGEMENT

You can get through a disaster without being destroyed by it. Your recovery can bring strength of character and compassion. While not all stories have happy endings, most victims will find great comfort in their faith. The compassion of volunteers who come to help bring both help and hope. It is most important to allow others to help. Accept the help of others who need to be needed. We can experience the goodness of others who work together to provide relief and recovery. Your local faith community can provide social and emotional support for everyone. Worship provides food for the soul as we gather to offer gratitude and joy for things that matter the most.

UNDERSTANDING THE SCRIPTURES

Read the following three scriptures out loud and answer these three brief questions:

Psalm 62:5-6; 2 Corinthians 4:3-4; Isaiah 40:31

What does the scripture say?

What does the scripture mean?

How does the scripture apply?

PRACTICAL APPLICATION

Goal 1: Be Prepared

Most people believe that with greater evidence of climate change it is important to be prepared. How can you be better prepared?

- What organization or local church will you support to help others?

- What funding can be raised through an emergency appeal?

- What are the immediate needs of the victims?

- What volunteer training will be used?

- What specialized mission or organizations like UMCOR will you partner with?

- How can you collaborate with districts, conferences, and other churches to make a more significant impact? (Most United Methodist Conferences have Volunteer in Ministry disaster coordinators who train and deploy volunteer teams.)

Goal 2: Listen

Listening is the best way to research how you can help. When you know the needs of those you are going to serve, you will be more effective.

- Ask questions.

- Listen to the local pastors and community leaders.
- Find out the most important needs.

Goal 3: Communicate Care

Short-term and long-term care is needed for relief and recovery following a disaster.

- Rely on God's spirit to guide your prayers and conversations. "The Holy Spirit will tell you at that very moment what you must say." (Luke 12:12)
- Encourage victims to cope and endure.
- Find small group opportunities, worship services, or other opportunities to offer tender love and care.

> You even showed sympathy toward people in prison and accepted the confiscation of your possessions with joy, since you knew that you had better and lasting possessions.
>
> —Hebrews 10:34

ACTION STEPS

As a volunteer or victim/survivor what steps will you now take? Check your top three:

___ Learn new coping skills

___ Reach out to others and offer your care

___ Connect with others through regular worship

___ Define yourself by who you are, not what you do

___ Be more aware of trauma symptoms

___ Count your blessings

___ Make each day count

___ Practice the power of gratitude and generosity

___ Serve the church as a volunteer in mission

___ Celebrate the social bonds that we can have through the unity that Christ brings us

Tools and Resources

Stephen B. Roberts and Willard W. C. Ashley Sr., eds., *Disaster Spiritual Care: Practical Clergy Resources to Community, Regional, and National Tragedy*, 2nd ed. (Nashville: SkyLight Paths, 2017).

Daniel P. Aldrich, *Building Resilience: Social Capital in Post-Disaster Recovery* (Chicago: University of Chicago Press, 2012).

John Trent and Gary Smalley, *The Blessing: Giving the Gift of Unconditional Love and Acceptance*, rev. ed. (Nashville: Thomas Nelson, 2011).

Harriet Hill, Margaret Hill, Dick Baggé, and Pat Miersma, *Healing the Wounds of Trauma: How the Church Can Help*, expanded ed. (Philadelphia: American Bible Society, 2016).

United Methodist Committee on Relief, (UMCOR), US Disaster Training, umcor.org.

The Salvation Army Emergency Disaster Services, disaster.salvation armyusa.org/training.

American Red Cross, redcross.org/take-a-class/disaster-training.

Heart to Heart International, Lenexa, Kansas, *After a Disaster Guidebook—How to Recover*, downloadable pdf or eBook. Also see, www.heart toheart.org.

Hurricane Harvey Disaster Recovery, Texas Annual Conference of The United Methodist Church, www.txcumc.org/disasterrecovery.

Chapter 8

FIVE TASKS FOR TRAUMA HEALING

You may be facing the perfect storm, but Jesus offers the perfect peace.
—Max Lucado

Group Study 2

Welcome and Introductions

Opening Prayer (spoken in unison)

> *Lord God, your love and assurance bring healing to our broken lives. Hear our laments, grant us continued strength and relief from pain. Guide us down the road to recovery trusting in your mercy every day. Help us rejoice in your goodness trusting in your daily blessings.*

Icebreaker Questions:

What one thing went well for you this week? What one thing did not?

Closing prayer

> *Bless us, Lord, with your deep patience, give us tranquility and peace as we turn daily to you in prayer. Grant us your perfect peace that passes our understanding. Amen.*

SYNOPSIS OF CHAPTER 2: RECOVERY— FIVE TASKS FOR TRAUMA HEALING

This chapter is all about recognizing and understanding the reality of your situation following the disaster. As you overcome your shock and accept your need for help, you can begin your road to recovery and healing from your trauma. Together, with others, this process can bring healing.

Review the five tasks of trauma healing and recovery:

1. Begin by taking a few simple steps to immediately cope with your situation.

2. Accept the reality of your loss and pain.

3. Find a safe place to express and experience your feelings and lament.

4. Recognize your need for faith in God's peace and purpose.

5. Help yourself by helping others.

Chapter 2 closes with a helpful inventory to measure the twelve practices that can help you grow through disaster. Be sure to check off those practices that needed continued attention for growth and healing. Write them down so you can measure your growth over the next few months or years. I would encourage you to do whatever it takes. Remember, each of us can find ways to improve by learning from our growth areas or even failures. One of my favorite professional golf commentators, David Feherty, puts it this way: "It's how you deal with failure that determines how you achieve success."

Key Discussion Questions

1. Which one of the above five tasks of trauma recovery do you think is the most difficult for you? Why?

2. How can the experience and practice of your personal faith bring you comfort, strength, and motivation?

3. How can this support group help you? And how can you help others in this group or in your family?

LESSONS FROM THE PAST

Two long years ago after the hurricane, I sat down on a curb near my home, sobbing, and asked God to help me. I was suicidal and I knew it. I wasn't sleeping, eating well, or functioning mentally. I was diagnosed with post-traumatic stress disorder. I was taking way too much medication.

I desperately didn't want to die. But I believed I was going to be one more fatality of the hurricane. I had always adored my wife and children. I was now fifty-seven years old. I was really depressed, and I did not want to live. I felt isolated. I would not talk to anyone.

I cried and begged God to help me...and one day when I had stopped taking the pills it seemed that the buzz in my head had gone away. I heard God speak to me. Suddenly, there was a silence. It sounded like an inner voice.

I hadn't prayed since I was a boy. I had made fun of God and those who loved God. And now, through my sobs, I heard myself begging and asking God to help me. I asked and I felt the Lord respond to me. I heard God in the silence, and I experienced an assurance. I felt God's love warm my cold and empty heart. I began to feel absolutely dependent on his help and forgiveness.

I didn't understand at first why the Lord gave me a sense of comfort and assurance. I didn't deserve Jesus's help, I thought. I was unworthy. I had ignored the Lord for forty years; why did he suddenly help me? It took me some time to understand that God helped me simply because he loves me. Because even though we don't deserve God's love, God loves us—all of us.

Not only did God give me the strength to be able to slowly overcome my post-traumatic stress disorder and depression, the Lord saved my life. I told my story to my wife's pastor. Then I told several of my friends who called this "a miracle." I just know that I was no longer so hurt and so angry at the hurricane that leveled my life.

I call it a miracle too. Why did God save the life of a man who had lived a very selfish life? The hurricane had blown away everything I had worked hard for my whole life. I no longer had my new car or my new house. But now I knew I had what was most important. Was it because my wife and I had two little boys we were trying to raise? Possibly. Maybe it was because of my wife's strong faith and trust in God. I did not know why. But I decided I did not need to know why. Instead, I wanted to know how I could trust God to help me now.

Group Discussion Questions

1. We know that trauma can overwhelm our normal ability to cope. What are some of the things that can hinder recovery (for example, fear, pride, impatience, lack of faith)?

2. How does God help those who feel they have lost purpose in life (read Psalm 34:18)?

3. What is our role in helping others who need encouragement and a desire to heal from their trauma?

WORDS OF ENCOURAGEMENT

Remember that prayer does not change God but it can change you and bring greater strength. Winston Churchill said, "Success is never failure. Failure is never fatal. It is courage that counts." You will gain greater confidence as you take one step at a time in the road to recovery. Asking God for help at the beginning of each day will guide you to do what is good. Take time throughout the day to pray, as it will help you recover your balance and create a new normal.

> This is the confidence that we have in our relationship with God: If we ask for anything in agreement with his will, he listens to us. If we know that he listens to whatever we ask, we know that we have received what we asked from him.
>
> —1 John 5:14-15

UNDERSTANDING THE SCRIPTURES

Read and reflect on these scriptures and questions.

Psalm 6:2-3: Can you identify with this lament? How would you describe your trauma?

Psalm 62:5-6: How does God's steadfast love offer comfort and hope in time of trial?

Psalm 22:1: Why is it helpful to ask God for answers when you do not understand?

Psalm 139:1-4: Does this verse assure you that God knows and understands you?

Jeremiah 29:11: In times of uncertainty how is this verse helpful?

One scripture among many had the most impact on my own grief recovery: Love puts up with all things, trusts in all things, hopes for all things, endures all things (1 Cor 13:7). I memorized this scripture and still say it almost daily. Scripture has helped me through surgeries and many other challenging life experiences.

> Find your key scripture.
> Memorize it to place it in your heart, mind, and soul.

ACTION STEPS

Most of us have symptoms of unhealed trauma wounds from the past. We may or may not remember them. We can continue to grieve our loss even though we function adequately in our work and personal relationships. Practicing prayer, medication, or quiet time on a regular basis is one of the best ways to find emotional and spiritual healing. You can do this individually or in a prayer group.

Ask yourself these questions:

1. What are areas that need attention and healing?

2. Who can partner with me as I share and pray for healing and hope?

3. How will attending worship on a regular basis help bring hope and healing?

4. What prayer-based exercises can I do to work out my painful feelings or burdens?

5. Which of the five tasks that bring healing and strength still need my attention and work?

Tools and Resources:

Bob Deitas Jr., *Life after Loss: A Practical Guide to Renewing Your Life after Experiencing Major Loss*, 6th ed. (Boston: Lifelong Books, 2017).

Kathryn M. Haueisen and Carol H. Flores, *A Ready Hope: Effective Disaster Ministry for Congregations* (Herndon, VA: Alban Institute, 2009).

Howard Clinebell Jr., *Well Being: A Personal Plan for Exploring and Enriching the Seven Dimensions of Life: Mind, Body, Spirit, Love, Work, Play, Earth* (Quezon City, Phillipines: Kadena Books, 1998).

Jack Alexander, *The God Guarantee: Finding Freedom from the Fear of Not Having Enough* (Grand Rapids, MI: Baker Books, 2017).

Rebuilding Hope after a Natural Disaster: Pathways to Emotional Healing and Recovery, Heart of Illinois United Way. Downloadable pdf at www. hoiunitedway.org/rebuilding-hope-after-a-natural-disaster/.

REIGNITING HOPE THROUGH LOVE

Theories and studies without regard for the refreshing virtue of God's order are merely dead letters, emptying the heart by filling the mind.
—Jean Pierre de Caussade

Group Study 3

Welcome and Introductions

Opening Prayer (spoken in unison)

> *Divine Physician, hear our prayers. Restore in us a pure heart, O Lord. You know us better than we know ourselves. We confess, Lord, that we wish we knew why this disaster happened. Help us discern how you are using this disaster to bring restoration. Help us not be bitter because we do not understand. But help us be better. Support and strengthen us as we reach out in love, concern, and care for others. Grant that we may always be blessed by your love that helps us bear all things, believe in your goodness, hope always, and endure by the power of your eternal love. We pray this through the one who makes all things new, Jesus Christ our Redeemer. Amen.*

Icebreaker Questions:

Some say that healing and finding comfort for our emotions may come before trying to understand why bad things happen. Is this true from your experience? What gives you the most hope?

SYNOPSIS OF CHAPTER 3: RESTORATION— REIGNITING HOPE

There are well over three hundred biblical references to *hope*. Biblical hope is based on God's promises and covenant. Hope is rooted in a deep sense of confidence. Hope gives us a powerful assurance of our salvation. The very nature of hope is based upon the love of God.

There are a number of biblically based characteristics of God's love that can inspire you and reignite your hope:

Love restores. (Eph 4:4)

Love suffers. (1 Pet 3:8)

Love seeks. (Prov 8:17)

Love transforms. (Rom 12:2)

Love heals. (Hos 14:4)

Love sustains. (*Wis.* 16:26)

Love is our anchor. (Heb 6:19)

Love is action. (Jer 7:3)

Love brings power to life. (Rom 15:13)

Key Discussion Questions

1. Which one of these hope-filled characteristics is most helpful to you now? Why?

2. People of faith are taught the very character of God is rooted in love. Why is this important to you?

3. If you have been a victim of a disaster, why would you then want to be of help to others?

LESSONS FROM THE PAST

Bruce Blumer, author of *Simply Grace*, shared in his blog entry "Why Do You Help?"[1] after serving with a disaster relief team in Texas after Hurricane Harvey in 2017. Bruce writes,

A week ago, I was part of a team that drove to Houston to help with the flood relief efforts. Let me begin with recognizing Cypress United Methodist Church in Cypress, Texas (in northwest Houston), who showed us incredible hospitality. Their pastors, staff, and the church have committed a tremendous amount of resources in hosting teams, reaching out, monitoring projects in homes, and assisting their community. At devotions one of the first nights, the team leader asked a question he too struggles with—why do you volunteer, why do you help? It prompted me to reflect on the reasons to help and my own motivations to drive thirty-two hours in a car and spend a week on my knees putting up sheetrock. I believe the reasons for helping are complex. When I asked the team to put in writing why they volunteered, here's a sampling of their responses:

- To serve others in need.

- First, to glorify and honor with thanksgiving to God. Second, to honor my family and my church with a thankful heart.

- The reason I volunteer is because I feel like I have been abundantly blessed by God and want to give back to show that I appreciate it. Also, I have had people come to my rescue when I needed it the most.

- I enjoy sharing my time and talents with others. The more I volunteer, the more drawn I feel toward volunteering again.

- Volunteering jump-starts my spiritual journey. A palpable sense of the Holy Spirit is with me when I am freely giving my time and talents to those in need.

My own reasons can be found in these responses too. I do feel I've been blessed and have the ability to help. I enjoy spending time with others, working toward a common goal. I feel good when I help and sometimes feel guilty for feeling that way. The more I volunteer, the more I volunteer. It helps me in my spiritual journey and energizes me.

Group Discussion Questions

1.   So why do you volunteer? Each of us may have our own reasons for help-ing others.

2.   Today, more and more people come to experience a deeper faith through mission work and involvement. Why do you think this is true?

3.   Bruce mentions a church that demonstrated incredible hospitality. How do churches in disaster areas witness God's love for victims and volunteers?

WORDS OF ENCOURAGEMENT

Look for ways to turn challenges into opportunities for recovery and restoration. Take time to notice people of faith around you who take the ordinary situations and add God's love in a way that becomes extraordinary. Know that disasters can dimin-ish your hope. How can you find help to reignite your hope? Recognize the power of a positive and can-do attitude. Realize that there are beliefs and myths that help or hurt. While bad things do happen in this world, out of those situations we see the amazing care of people who come to our aid. Trust yourself, others, and especially the hope that comes from God. You can grow through your grief and loss to recognize lasting values. Live your life and leave a legacy of love, faith, and hope.

UNDERSTANDING THE SCRIPTURES

Read each scripture aloud and answer the questions for each passage:
1 Chronicles 28:20; Romans 8:28; Galatians 2:20

What does this scripture say?

What does this scripture mean?

How does this scripture apply?

PRACTICAL APPLICATION

It is all about hope. How does hope help you? Does your hope give you strength and resilience? Why do we see some people handle trauma and loss better than others? Is it because they have had less trauma and loss, or are there other reasons? How does our faith factor increase your capacity for hope? And how can you grow stronger after a crisis so that you can better handle the next crisis? We can see how hope brings greater strength to not only survive a disaster but also grow emotionally and thrive spiritually.

Here are a few myths about hope:

Myth 1: Hope means your troubles will go away.

Myth 2: Hope is something we always feel.

Myth 3: Hope is easily lost in troubled times.

What other myths about hope can you identify? Consider these four helpful characteristics about hope:

Hope helps us handle adversity and gives us a perspective of meaning and purpose.

Hope can become a source of strength when our emotions need comfort or control.

Hope offers Christians connections that guide outreach to help others.

Hope motivates you to take better care of yourself, your body, your mind, and your soul.

What other characteristics of hope can you identify?

ACTION STEPS

1. Know what hopeful steps you can begin to take to keep on going.

2. Recognize that every challenge may also bring an opportunity, not just a difficulty.

3. Gain greater trust in a biblically based hope. Highlight passages and then memorize them.

4. Identify and commit yourself to your life goals daily through prayer and meditation.

5. Know your limitations and control those things you can control.

6. Express gratitude often to God and others.

Tools and Resources

Adam Hamilton, *Unafraid: Living with Courage and Hope in Uncertain Times* (New York: Convergent Books, 2018).

Max Lucado, *Anxious for Nothing: Finding Calm in a Chaotic World* (Nashville: HarperCollins, 2017).

Arlene K. Unger, *Calm: 50 Mindfulness and Relaxation Exercises to De-Stress and Unwind* (New York: Metro Books, 2015).

William Barclay, *Prayers for Help and Healing* (Minneapolis, MN: Augsburg, 1968).

John Wimber, Kevin Springer, and Richard J. Foster, *Power Healing*, 2nd ed. (Nashville: HarperCollins, 1987).

Jane Cage, ed. *Joplin Pays It Forward: An Essay Collection of Lessons Learned*. Download a pdf or purchase an eBook at http://janecage .com/joplin-pays-it-forward/. Joplin, Missouri, was the site of one of the deadliest tornadoes in US history on May 22, 2011. This collection of essays by community leaders shares the recovery process and offers advice to civic leaders.

Chapter 10

RECOVERING YOUR FINANCIAL LIFE

*Just as we develop our physical muscles through overcoming opposition—
such as lifting weights—we develop our character muscles
by overcoming challenges and adversity.*

—Stephen Covey

Group Study 4

Welcome and Introductions

Opening Prayer (spoken in unison)

> *Dear Lord, As we embark on the work of healing our financial lives,
> please give us the wisdom to do what is best and right, courage to face
> the task at hand, and patience to wait on you as we work through this
> time of testing. Thank you for your good gifts and your mercy that has
> brought us this far. We acknowledge that you are the source of all our
> provision. Please give us our daily bread and a double portion of your
> Spirit. Amen.*

Icebreaker Questions:

When you think about what you have lost, what are you having the most difficulty
dealing with (job, income, home, personal effects [photos, mementos, family heir-
looms])?

Despite the personal tragedy you are facing, can you name something you are thankful for?

SYNOPSIS OF CHAPTER 4: ASSESSMENT— TAKING YOUR FINANCIAL PULSE

In chapter 4 we looked at the importance of taking a financial assessment to determine our current financial status and help us assess which areas are requiring the most attention in our financial recovery. We answered several key questions about our current cash flow, job status, personal data/records, and availability of credit cards and systems so that we could determine our next steps. The post-disaster checklist will also assist you in taking the necessary steps to begin building your overall financial recovery plan.

In this small group session we will work to accomplish the following objectives:

Take our financial pulse so that we can prioritize what we need to work on first to begin our financial recovery.

Identify relief resources from the government or nonprofit sector to provide immediate assistance if not being used.

Encourage one another to begin digging out and building a more substantial plan for the financial part of our recovery.

Key Discussion Questions

1. Knowing everyone's situation will be different, what are the key resources you need right now to begin your recovery process?

2. What government or nonprofit resources can you tap into immediately?

   How or where can you get both financial and emotional support to help you and your family navigate this daunting task of recovery from a natural or personal disaster?

3. Look back at your score on the financial checkup from earlier in the book. How would you rate your overall financial situation right now on a scale of 1–10, with 10 being the best score?

LESSONS FROM THE PAST

Anne's entire marriage was traumatic, financially and emotionally fractured almost from day one. Ben would not hold down a job, and he repeatedly made terrible financial decisions. All the financial pressure fell back on Anne to support their family, which is a lot for any twentysomething to manage. Being a health-care worker, not surprisingly, she was good at taking care of people, and she made a Herculean effort to hold it all together despite Ben's abuses. His drug rehab was expensive, and so were the legal costs from trying to navigate two separations after more than a decade of struggle. In a bizarre twist, the judge would not order Ben out of their house because *he* didn't have a job and could not support himself, even though he was clearly hurting Anne and their kids with his destructive behavior and refusal to work. Because of the kids and her desire to honor scripture, Anne agonized over the decision to divorce, but the hardships, mistreatments, and manipulations mounted. Ben continued to rack up credit card debt while floating in and out of jobs. When Ben's and their kids' bank accounts were cleared out by creditors due to his financial mismanagement, the stark reality hit that he would never change. Anne recognized that scripture also instructs us to guard our hearts above all else because our heart is the wellspring of life. Her heart was crushed. A wise and loving family member and spiritual advisor took Anne aside and encouraged her to reclaim her life and end the cycle of abuse, for the sake of her heart and her kids' hearts. It was time.

As is often the sad case in divorce, the woman is so desperate to extricate herself from the abuse she is going through that she accepts an unfavorable settlement. However Anne turned to the Lord anew and trusted God to lead her. Remarkably, she found a good lawyer willing to take an uber-reasonable flat fee of $2,000 to handle the proceedings. Ben stalled and raged and was petulant, but she avoided a costly trial in exchange for a more favorable arrangement. She would not have to pay alimony (incredulous as that may sound in light of his neglect), in exchange for a one-time payment. And she was free. Not to say that it was easy. She had to turn over half of her retirement account from work, nearly $100,000. However, the journey from financial trauma to financial healing had begun.

As they often do, the blessings came as she walked in obedience. Anne had a good job so she could support herself. A friend rented her a room for next to nothing to help her get back on her feet. The biggest challenge, after marrying at such a young age, was the reality that she was now truly on her own, having to make big life decisions. Despite Ben's poor financial choices, Anne's credit thankfully remained undamaged, and within a year and a half she felt that financially she was moving past the trauma. She invested heavily in Christian counseling, and her divorce care group at church was a lifeline for her spiritual recovery. God truly met Anne in the valley, and carried her through the trauma to a new life in him.

Group Discussion Questions

1. What can you do if you don't have any emergency funds to help you face your situation?

2. Are there other accounts you own that you could gain access to such as a loan from a 401(k), hardship distribution from another retirement plan; or a distribution from an IRA or college savings plan?

   Note: We realize there may be penalties or negative tax consequences for pulling funds from a retirement or college account. Please consult your tax advisor or financial planner first so you understand the full implications of this last-resort option.

3. What have you or others found helpful in terms of government assistance, faith-based programs, or resources provided by local businesses or your employer?

WORDS OF ENCOURAGEMENT

Time, patience, and perseverance—three things we often feel short on even in the best of times. We pray God's grace will be sufficient for you and meet your every care as you daily entrust to him your every need. A terrible and devastating thing has happened, and you will likely need a significant amount of time, patience, and perseverance to see you through. Hopefully it is helpful to remember that there are many others in your same situation. You are not alone! Using the resources in this small group session, we encourage you to reach out to others so that can carry each other's burdens and heal personally and as a community.

UNDERSTANDING THE SCRIPTURES

Read the scripture below aloud, and then discuss the questions that follow.

The thief enters only to steal, kill, and destroy.

I came so that they could have life—

indeed, so that they could live life to the fullest. (John 10:10)

1. In light of your financial trauma, what does "living life to the fullest" or living abundantly look like to you now? Has your opinion on this changed since before your setback?

2. Money issues and challenges often bring fear into our lives. How are you managing any financial fears you may now be facing?

3. Think about how you have managed your money over the years. Do you feel that the approach you used in the past has led you to an abundant life? Are there places God may be asking you to make changes?

PRACTICAL APPLICATION

List three areas you want/need to focus on in the next two weeks to begin to rebuild your financial world.

1. _____

2. _____

3. _____

List three goals you would like to accomplish in the next one to two months in your rebuilding/recovery process.

1. _____

2. _____

3. _____

Discussion Questions

1. What is the biggest challenge facing you right now in light of the financial trauma you have just experienced?

2. Based on how you scored on your financial checkup earlier in the book, share one thing you need help with to make progress.

3. What resources do you need to help you begin to overcome the setbacks or challenges you are facing? Do you have ideas to share with the group that may help others?

4. How do you see God at work in the midst of this tragedy? What encouragement do you have to share with the group to give others a glimpse of God's light in a dark moment?

ACTION STEPS

Consider the following action steps to help you start your financial recovery process:

Step 1—To gain perspective on what is happening with your finances, consider tracking all your expenses this week as part of your plan to determine where your money is going. Use either a written ledger or phone app to record each expense. If you make this a habit, tracking expenses will help you live out Proverbs 27:23.

Step 2—Enlist the help of a financial coach to direct your recovery process with money management. A coach can provide insight, encouragement, and accountability.

PREPARATION FOR NEXT SESSION: ESTABLISHING YOUR EMERGENCY MONEY MANAGEMENT PLAN

Complete these steps to prepare for the next *Growing through Disaster* small group session.

Read the following scripture passages and answer the questions below.

Proverbs 27:23-24; Proverbs 30:7-9.

Spend some time in prayer asking God, "What are you specifically trying to teach me about money and possessions during this trial/challenge?" What do you hear the Lord saying? Write any insights on the lines provided.

_____

_____

_____

Tools and Resources

Matt Schoenfeld, *Abundant Living: The Five Biblical Principles for Financial Success* (self-pub., Vibrant Group, 2005).

Expense tracking information: https://mattschoenfeld44.wixsite.com /abundantlivingmin/product-page/expense-tracking-sheets.

Chapter 11

BUILDING YOUR MONEY MANAGEMENT PLAN

*The real measure of your wealth is how much you'd be worth
if you lost all your money.*

—*Anonymous*

Group Study 5

Opening Prayer (spoken in unison)

*Heavenly Father, please give us the wisdom and knowledge to
manage money your way. Help us to use the resources you have
provided to us to build your kingdom, show love to ourselves and our
family, and meet our daily needs. Give us new insight into better
ways to manage our money. Please teach us about money and how
it works. As we work to rebuild our financial worlds due to the
disasters we have faced, please help us to lean on you and trust you.
Please help us in our time of need. In the name of the one true God,
Jesus, Amen.*

Welcome and Introductions

Icebreaker Questions:

Has anything new hit you this week that is affecting your financial recovery? What help do you need to address the concern?

What has been your past experience trying to use a budget? Did it work? Why or why not?

What do you think will happen to your situation if you begin tracking where you spend your money?

SYNOPSIS OF CHAPTER 5— MONEY MANAGEMENT STRATEGIES

In chapter 5, we introduced five core biblical principles for successful money management. These principles are designed to work in conjunction with each other to form your money management foundation. As you work to recover from your financial trauma, focusing on the five principles will give you a simple roadmap for healing your financial life and lead you to a place of deeper financial discipleship. These biblical imperatives will help you break free from our culture of quick riches and the endless quest for more.

Five Biblical Principles for Financial Recovery™

Give generously. (2 Cor 9:6-8)

Flee the love of money. (1 Tim 6:9-12)

Live within your means. (Prov 30:8-9)

Plan for the future. (Luke 14:28)

Use a spending plan. (Prov 27:23-24)

The Bible includes a treasure trove of practical wisdom to help us be more effective at managing the resources that God places in our hands. If we give generously, we will be freed from the clutches of materialism and acknowledge our faith in God's provision by giving our money back to the Giver. By fleeing the love of money, we will learn contentment and gratitude. As we explored the more practical principles, we devised a plan to live within our means, spending less than we make each month, so that we build margin in our finances to save and give. As we follow the biblical call to plan for the future, we partner with God to responsibly prepare for what may come with an attitude of faith. Finally, we learned from the wisdom of Proverbs that having a monthly plan to manage our personal finances is a biblical concept that will lead us to take care of business now and be able to bless generations to come. Following this key wisdom from scripture will enable us to build a realistic plan to guide us as we recover from financial disaster.

In this small group session we will work to accomplish the following objectives:

- Build your personal monthly spending plan to follow as a guide to rebuilding your financial life.

- Encourage one another to follow the Five Biblical Principles for Financial Recovery™,

- Learn contentment as we grow in our faith that God will meet our every need in Christ Jesus.

Key Discussion Questions

1. After reviewing the Five Biblical Principles for Financial Recovery,™ discuss the benefits and challenges of being a steward. Which of these principles seems hardest for you to follow?

2. Based on your current financial challenges, how could these five principles support your recovery process?

3. In the parable of the talents, the master actually takes the lone talent from the unfaithful manager and gives it to the manager who had the most. Does that seem backward? Why would God give more resources to the one who had the greatest amount of resources? What does this tell us about how God views money management?

LESSONS FROM THE PAST

A long time ago, a certain word was frequently used to describe a person who took care of someone else's financial affairs. This person was called a steward. Today we might call this person a business manager or even an accountant. However, these labels may be too limited, for the influence of a steward was more far-reaching. The definition of the word *steward* is very significant for every follower of Jesus. According to Webster's, a steward is one who is employed to manage domestic concerns such as collecting rents, keeping accounts, and directing servants. A steward was in charge of a boss's entire household and business affairs. While a steward does not own any of the money he or she is managing, he or she is entrusted with the job of making sure his or her boss's affairs are in good order.

A modern-day example of a steward comes from the world of investing. Today, one out of every two Americans owns shares of a mutual fund. A mutual fund is an investment vehicle where thousands of investors pool their money, and then a professional money manager is hired to take the money and invest it in a portfolio of stocks or bonds. The portfolio manager acts as the steward, managing the investors' money with the goal of creating a competitive return on investment.

This is exactly what God asks of us. He has provided us with a variety of resources (finances, talents, relationships, and time), and we have the job of taking care of them and investing them for the purpose of building his kingdom. This is the foundational principle that underlies everything we will learn in this study about how the Lord wants us to manage money: God owns it; we manage it. Even in a time of crisis, the principles for biblical financial success, and our role to manage God's money, do not change. The challenge may be a little harder, and the resources may be temporarily scarcer, but the job we have is the same. Take good care of God's money and believe his promise that he will take care of us.

In James 1:17, we are taught that "Every good and perfect gift is from above, coming down from the Father of heavenly lights" (NIV). God is the creator, and therefore, the owner of all things, and that includes money. He made it, and in his goodness and generosity, he has provided each of us with a portion to manage while we serve him on earth. The challenge we constantly face is deciding if we will manage what he's given us according to his principles for his glory. One way we can show our love for God is through obeying his commands, even when they are not easy. Those commands are for our good so that we can overcome the financial challenges that have been dealt to us by this crisis. Under your current circumstances, this obedience may include extra work hours to get on your feet, limiting expenses to the absolute minimum until your situation can stabilize, saving any extra if at all possible because you will likely face uncertainties for weeks or months to come, planning, and giving on some level back to God's work as a way to thank him for carrying you through this trial.

Group Discussion Questions

1. It can seem like a foreign concept in our "me-culture" to think that the money or possessions I own are, in fact, not my own. How have the financial challenges you are going through changed your view of money and possessions?

2. Read Psalm 24:1. How does a person go from believing "This is my money" to "This is God's money"?

3. How does the act of giving impact our ability to turn our money over to God?

4. Proverbs 27:23-24 has a lot to say about money management. "Be sure you know the condition of your flocks, give careful attention to your herds; for riches do not endure forever, and a crown is not secure for all generations" (NIV). What stands out to you the most as you read these verses?

WORDS OF ENCOURAGEMENT

You can do this! We pray the money management tools in this study will give you new confidence and practical aid to tackle your situation. This quote from the famed Dale Carnegie is encouraging: "Develop success from failures. Discouragement and failure are two of the surest stepping stones to success." Use the Five Biblical Principles for Financial Recovery™ to lead you to stronger financial footing, and then keep using them in years to come to guide your financial life. A long-term benefit from your current setback may well be newfound financial contentment.

UNDERSTANDING THE SCRIPTURES

Read Matthew 25:14-30 aloud, and then discuss the questions.

What are the consequences before God for how we manage our money?

Based on Jesus's teaching in Matthew 25, what could we do differently to improve our situation if we feel we are short on resources?

PRACTICAL APPLICATION

Building your personal two-part spending plan

Follow this five-step process listed below to begin building your personal spending plan. Refer back to chapter 5 if you need a refresher on spending plans. Use the spending plan worksheet provided below to build your personal financial recovery plan.

Step 1: List the amount of income you are bringing in each month—after taxes.

Note: Remember, in the early stages of your financial crisis, your goal is to meet the basic needs of daily living (food, clothing, shelter, transportation). You may have categories on the sheet where you list no expenditures for now. As your situation improves, you may begin to add more to your normal expense categories.

Step 2: Estimate how much you will spend in each spending category and enter a target for the month.

Step 3: Add all expenses and ensure the monthly expense total is less than or equal to your projected income.

Step 4: Track where you are spending your money each month (use a written log, spreadsheet, or a phone app, based on your preference). Each week add up what you have spent in each category so you can check to see if you are on track for your overall monthly targets in step 2. (Complete step 4 outside of group time.)

Step 5: Adjust your plan as necessary if income is more or less, or if you have an issue with any expense categories. By tracking each week, you will have a better understanding of where your money is being spent, and it should help you make changes as needed so that your outflow does not exceed your income. (Complete step 5 outside of group time.)

Note: In the early stages of your financial crisis, you may need to rely on a credit card to cover expenses until a later time when life has calmed down. This is normal and may be your only source for covering needs. Just be aware of interest charges and late fees, and be in contact with your card company to see if they will waive those charges in light of the situation.

Practical Application Discussion

1. Were you able to build a workable spending plan for the coming month? What other help do you need?

2. Based on your spending plan, what do you foresee will be your biggest challenges. Work together on ideas to help find solutions.

3. Tracking expenses and adjusting your plan weekly are the keys to a successful spending plan. What method for tracking expenses do you think will work best for your situation?

4. If you are projecting to bring in less than you are spending, what is your plan to narrow or erase that gap?

ACTION STEPS

Consider the following action steps to help you start your financial recovery process:

Step 1: Continue tracking your expenses during the week. Jot down any insights you have as a result and be ready to share with your group.

Step 2: Write down a list of all your assets (value of bank accounts, investments, vehicles, home, and other valuables like jewelry or antiques). Also make a list of all your debts. Having this list will show you your strengths and weaknesses financially and should help you in recovery decision making. Knowing your overall position is an important first step. Use the Net Worth Planning Sheet in Appendix A. Assessing your net worth helps you determine the overall strength of your finances and identify areas that may need to work.

PREPARATION FOR NEXT SESSION: PLANNING FOR RECOVERY

Complete these steps to prepare for the next *Growing through Disaster* small group session.

Read the following scripture passages: 1 Timothy 6:6-8; Philippians 4:11-13.

Begin thinking about short-term and long-term financial goals you wish to accomplish.

Tools and Resources

Matt Schoenfeld, *Abundant Living: The Five Biblical Principles for Financial Success* (self-pub., Vibrant Group, 2005).

Matt Schoenfeld, *Managing Your Money: Principles for Abundant Living* (Kansas City, MO: Beacon Hill, 2008).

Intuit Mint is a bill pay and budget management software: www.mint.com.

PocketGuard is a personal finance application: https://pocketguard.com/.

Federal Emergency Management Agency (FEMA): 1-800-621-3362; www.fema.gov/.

To find local, state, and other resources in your area and a map that shows currently declared disaster areas, go to www.disasterassistance.gov.

PLANNING FOR YOUR FINANCIAL FUTURE

*Gratitude makes sense of our past, brings peace for today,
and creates a vision for tomorrow.*
—Melody Beattie

Obedient preparation often precedes blessings.
—Matt Schoenfeld

Group Study 6

Opening Prayer (spoken in unison)

> *Dear Lord, In times of trial and adversity, please draw us to you.
> Where there is anxiety, give us peace. Where there is fear, give us
> faith. Where there is despair, give us hope. Where there is weakness,
> give us courage. Please send your Holy Spirit to comfort, guide, and
> heal those who have faced great loss, hurt, and pain. Grant us the
> grace to face today, knowing your love will sustain us and lead us
> into peace that passes all understanding. Thank you, Father, for your
> limitless mercy. Give us a vision for tomorrow. Help us to plan wisely
> and prepare to the best of our ability to face the coming days. Guide
> us into your presence so that we may know true peace. Amen.*

Welcome and Introductions

Icebreaker Questions:

Share a time when you failed to plan and it resulted in a negative consequence.
What did this experience teach you?

Now share the opposite: a time when you had prepared and you saw the benefit of being ready. How did this experience differ from the first?

Do you have a trusted friend or a financial advisor who can assist you in building a more extensive financial recovery plan? Share any thoughts on what you will focus on next to develop your plan.

SYNOPSIS OF CHAPTER 6—PLANNING YOUR FINANCIAL RECOVERY PLAN

In light of our need to have complete faith and trust in God, the Bible has a lot to say about our need to plan ahead in life. As you begin to piece your life back together after the trauma you have experienced, chapter 6 focuses on building simple plans to help you set manageable goals so you begin to make progress. Examples are provided for how to create a short-term recovery plan if you need to focus on the basics like food, clothing, and shelter. Once in place, thought is given to building week by week, and then monthly plans for recovery. A helpful checklist is also provided for dealing with insurance, FEMA (if you are a natural disaster victim), and contractors (if you face rebuilding).

Additionally, in an effort to assist you in being prepared as possible for the next emergency situation you may face, we introduce the concept of a grab and go emergency kit. This emergency preparedness kit contains a digital copy of all your important personal and legal documents, other key financial items, and a small supply of food, water, and medical supplies. For those who have perhaps already lost their home, we realize the kit may no longer be possible to build; however, in time it will be a wise tool for everyone to prepare.

To close out the chapter, we explore the longer-range financial planning task of building your personal legacy plan. Flipping the script from "estate planning," which may carry a boring, stodgy, or even overwhelming connotation, we introduce the idea of your "legacy of love plan." By planning in advance we are able to show love to God and family by mapping out how we will steward our possessions from this life once we are gone. Seven important legal and financial documents are introduced that all people need to have, and a deeper look into the differences between having a will and a trust are clearly mapped out so that we can make an informed decision about how each of us can build the best legacy of love plan for our situation.

In this small group session we will work to accomplish the following objectives:

Get encouraged and inspired to begin looking at the next stage of your financial recovery and the steps you can take once this study is completed to continue growing through disaster.

Examine the importance of planning in the Christian life in general and for your recovery process.

Build an immediate and intermediate-range financial plan to aid recovery from your personal financial trauma.

Key Discussion Questions

1. Rate yourself on a scale of 1–10 (10 as the highest score) at how proficient you are at planning for your financial future. Share why you gave yourself that score.

2. Planning may seem difficult right now with all you have been through or are currently experiencing. Jeremiah 29:11 says, "'For I know the plans I have for you,' declares the LORD, 'plans to prosper you and not to harm you, plans to give you hope and a future'" (NIV). Do you see areas where God is moving to rebuild your life and give you a future hope?

3. Planning can bring a sense of structure to life, which you may currently find very attractive if you sense a level of chaos in your financial world due to your trauma. At this phase, what type of plan do you need most: short-term, intermediate-term, or longer-term? Why?

LESSONS FROM THE PAST

This is what the LORD says: "Make this valley full of ditches."
For this is what the LORD says: "You will see neither wind nor rain,
yet this valley will be filled with water,
and you, your cattle and your other animals will drink."
—*2 Kings 3:16-17 (NIV)*

Mark had been "digging ditches" for years. Like 2 Kings 3 teaches (see above), he had tried to do the work necessary to plan as best he could if a tight stretch ever were to come. In an effort to prudently plan for the future, he had been stashing away some money every so often so that he and his wife, Candace, and their son, Brett, would have a healthy emergency fund. Just in case.

Mark had tried to listen to the wisdom in God's Word that told him the prudent man prepares for the winter seasons of life that will inevitably come. Once their second baby was born, it was a lot harder to keep putting money aside. There were diapers and clothes and medicine to buy. But by this time, their emergency fund totaled about $11,000. A healthy cushion.

And then it happened. Mark unexpectedly lost his job at

---

the large telecommunications company where he had worked for many years. He was laid off with only three weeks' severance pay. And they had just bought a new car! Great timing. It was small consolation that he was not alone. His whole division was nearly wiped out, and many of his co-workers were in a state of panic. Now he knew why he'd been digging those ditches all those years. Losing his job was devastating to him. It was a real blow to his confidence. What did the Lord have for him and his family? He sure was thankful for that emergency fund now.

It took Mark nearly eight months to find a new job. In the meantime, the Lord provided side jobs, gifts from friends, and a part-time job for Candace. The new job was a much better fit for Mark, and at the end of the day, he felt God had used this turn of events to deepen his faith and put him into a better position to use his gifts and skills. Plus, he'd gotten to spend a lot of extra time with his kids, which turned out to be an unexpected, but added, blessing.

Make no mistake—it was not the easiest or most pleasant process, but the emergency fund carried them through and helped his family avoid a major financial disaster. Mark was also convinced that by planning ahead and saving for a down time, he actually had done a very loving thing for his family. Mark and Candace were both so thankful that God had provided abundantly for their needs—through their emergency savings and the support of their friends and family.

Group Discussion Questions

1. Mark had the benefit of planning ahead for his emergency. What can you do if you don't have any emergency funds to help you face your situation?

2. As you begin to rebuild your financial world, what do you want to do differently to help you be better prepared for the next financial emergency you may face?

3. Sound planning and goal setting can take focus, time, and prayer. How does planning for the future make us more loving and supportive of our family?

WORDS OF ENCOURAGEMENT

As we wrap up this small group and you embark on life post financial trauma, we want to encourage you to do two main things:

1. Continue to meet with at least a couple of people who can encourage you and hold you accountable as you try to rebuild. The Lord does not intend for us to go it alone—life is always better when lived in community. Seek out fellowship.

2. Take it slow and steady. Don't worry if it takes you a while to get things back in order. It's okay to have failures and setbacks. True success does not mean that everything goes perfectly and you never hit a stumbling block. Success is found when you keep growing and trusting God even when life is not perfect. Don't give up hope; God is near to the brokenhearted!

UNDERSTANDING THE SCRIPTURES

Read Matthew 2:13-15 aloud and discuss the questions that follow.

1. In this passage, we see Joseph also had a traumatic decision to make. Certainly, it was life changing. In what ways would suddenly moving to Egypt affect the family finances? Do you see any parallels to your situation?

2. While Joseph had divine leading for this significant life change, how did he also rely on planning?

3. How else does the Lord use or reinforce the idea of planning in other parts of the Bible?

PRACTICAL APPLICATION

In our first small group session, you began to think about some basic planning tactics for the coming weeks. Now we wish to expand on those plans and create more specific goals and strategies to aid you in your financial recovery. The following areas are a starting point of issues you may be dealing with depending on your situation:

Food acquisition

Clothing

Housing arrangements

Transportation options

Monthly cash flow

Dealing with your job

Dealing with insurance or legal matters

As you look over this list, select the areas that are impacting you the most as you build your plans below. If you feel you have progressed beyond the immediate-term plan, start with the level that best meets your needs. As you work on the plans, help each other and share ideas, as some may be further along than others, or some may be more adept at planning. Bear one another's burdens and provide encouragement and support to your group. Above all, please don't feel like these plans, or any other exercises in the book for that matter, have to be perfect or 100 percent complete. Get something down on paper now to begin the process, but revisit and update your plans as needed or as circumstances change. You may want to select an accountability partner you can keep meeting with to help each other stay on track. Our goal is to provide a simple tool to get you started.

Practical Application Discussion

1. We realize it may take more time to fully develop your plan. What else do you need at this point to formulate a more complete/effective plan?

2. What task on your plan would you say is the most important thing you could accomplish to help your situation? What is your target date to get it completed by?

3. The legacy of love plan discussed in chapter 6 is easy to avoid yet critically important. Do you have resources at work or church that can help you set these up (prepaid legal benefit through your job's benefit program or a financial workshop at church)?

Financial Planning Worksheet
(to complete over the next 2–3 weeks)

NEXT WEEK

Objective	Goal	Finish-by Date	Check-off Box

BY END OF THE MONTH

Objective	Goal	Finish-by Date	Check-off Box

BY END OF QUARTER (in three months)

Objective	Goal	Finish-by Date	Check-off Box

ACTION STEPS

Consider the following action steps to help you start your financial recovery process:

Step 1: Develop a written long-range plan. Writing down goals and plans is powerful and tends to increase your chances of executing those objectives. Expand upon the shorter-range plans we have helped you with in this session. Work with your spouse (if married) or a trusted friend to encourage each other to take this step.

Step 2: If you need more help, enlist the services of a trusted financial advisor or financial coach. You will be surprised how many people are honored to be asked to help, and how much more effective you will be by having more than one brain on the job. See the resources section for how you can locate an advisor or coach.

Step 3: Above all else, seek God's leading for your plans. As our theme verse stated, God has plans for us. Be sure to seek his kingdom first and sync your plans to where God is leading you. Write down your prayers and answers to prayers as you work through your recovery. Then you can reflect back and see God's faithfulness and see his hand moving in your recovery process.

MOVING FORWARD—HELPING OTHERS

Now that you have completed the *Growing through Disaster* small groups, consider how you might help others who are not as far along as you are in the recovery process. Here are a couple of ideas to pray about:

Start a new small group and lead the participants through this six-week program.

Talk with your pastor or other community leaders about ways you can serve and give as you continue your journey of growing through disaster.

Serve as a financial coach or lead a grief/trauma recovery group.

Tools and Resources

Elmer L. Towns, *Fasting for Financial Breakthrough: A Guide to Uncovering God's Perfect Plan for Your Finances* (Bloomington, MN: Bethany House, 2002).

Kingdom Advisors, a Christian financial advisor network: https://kingdom advisors.com/find-a-professional/directory-search.

Directory of Dave Ramsey-endorsed financial coaches in your area: www.daveramsey.com/coaching#Coaching-cta.

FEMA Emergency Financial First Aid Kit (EFFAK), downloadable pdf: www.fema.gov/media-library/assets/documents/96123/financial -preparedness.

ADDITIONAL RECOVERY TOOLS

Recovery Spending Plan

Income

Total income after taxes/benefits: $_____

Expenses

Giving $_____

Housing/Utilities $_____

Food $_____

Clothing $_____

Transportation $_____

Medical/Insurance $_____

Household/Personal $_____

Entertainment $_____

Professional Expenses $_____

Saving/Investment $_____

Debts $_____

Other: _____ $_____

Other: _____ $_____

Total Expenses $_____

Surplus/Deficit $_____

Financial Net Worth

Net worth is the value that is left over when you subtract any money you owe from the total value of your assets.

Net Worth = Total Assets –Total Debts

Net worth is important because it gives you a snapshot of your financial situation on a given day. Determining net worth will often help us identify problem areas in our finances such as debt issues or lack of saving or planning. It is also a way to take our financial pulse and gauge our progress year-to-year.

Target Net Worth

The following formula will help you determine your target net worth.

Target Net Worth = Annual salary x (Age / 10)

For example:

A forty-year-old is making $50,000 a year.

$50,000 x (40 / 10) *or* $50,000 x 4 = $200,000 target net worth

For married couples who both earn income, combine incomes and average your ages.

Husband (age 35) with an annual salary of $42, 000

Wife (age 38) with an annual salary of $42,000

$84,000 x [((35 + 38) / 2) / 10] or $84,000 x (36.5 / 10) = combined *target* net worth

$84,000 x 3.65 = $306,600 = $306,600 target net worth

My Target Net Worth Worksheet

My annual salary $ _____

Spouse's annual salary $ _____

Total annual salary: $ _____

My age: _____

If you have a spouse, calculate the average of the two ages to use in the formula:

Your age   _____

Spouse's age   _____

    Combined ages   _____

    Average age (Combined ages /2)   _____

(Total salary: $ _____) x (Age: ___ / 10) = $ _____ (target net worth)

What I Owe (Debt)

Credit Cards	Balance due	Interest Rate	Monthly Payment	Final Pay- ment Date
Visa				
Visa				
MasterCard				
MasterCard				
Discover				
American Express				
Department Store				
Department Store				
Gas Card				
Gas Card				
Other				
Other				
Other				

Other Loans	Balance due	Interest Rate	Monthly Payment	Final Payment Date
Credit Union				
Car Loan				
Car Loan				
Bank Loan				
Bank Loan				
Finance Company				
Furniture/ Appliances				
Student Loans				
Other				
Other				
Other				
Other				
Other				
Home Mortgage				

Total: **Credit Card Debt:** $ _____

              Other Loans: $ _____

Total Debt: $ _____

What I Own (Assets)

Liquid:

Checking Account	$_____
Savings Account	$_____
Money Market Accounts	$_____
Certificate of Deposits	$_____
Stocks & Mutual Funds	$_____
Bonds	$_____
Insurance (cash value)	$_____
_____	$_____
_____	$_____
Total Liquid Assets:	**$_____**

Non-Liquid:

Home (market value)	$_____
Car (market value)	$_____
Car (market value)	$_____
IRAs	$_____
Retirement Plans	$_____
Furniture	$_____
Jewelry	$_____
Loans Receivable	$_____
_____	$_____
_____	$_____
Total Non-Liquid Assets:	**$_____**
Total Assets:	**$_____**

My Net Worth
(Assets - Debts = Net Worth)

Total Assets	−	Total Debts	=	Net Worth
$	−	$	=	$

My Financial Net Worth Statement—Year-to-Year Comparison

ASSETS	12.31.___ (current year)	12.31.___	12.31.___	12.31.___	12.31.___
Cash Assets					
Cash					
Checking					
Money Markets					
Receivables					
Stocks/ Bonds					
Other					
Other					
Total Cash Assets					
Long-Term Assets					
Art/ Jewelry					
Car 1					
Car 2					
Computers					
College Fund					
Home					

House Furnishings					
Mutual Funds					
Retirement savings					
Other					
Other					
Total Long-Term Assets					
TOTAL ASSETS					
LIABILITIES					
Credit Cards					
Car Loan					
Furniture Loan					
Mortgage					
Other Loan					
Other Loan					
TOTAL LIABILITIES					
NET WORTH					
Percentage Increase					
Amount Increase					

DISASTER RECOVERY GROUP GUIDELINES

Happy are people who show mercy, because they will receive mercy.
—Matthew 5:7

Recovery from trauma and loss is an active process of growth, not passive waiting. The small group process is a dynamic, prayerful, and supportive process that builds relationships of trust and care.

Recovery Groups can also be helpful to those dealing with serious illness, death, loss of employment, divorce, and other losses.

For the Participants and Facilitator:

Here are a few suggested guidelines or small group rules the group can consider and approve:

1. Start and stop on time. Turn cell phones off.

2. Everyone has an opportunity to participate in discussion.

3. Confidentiality matters.

4. It is okay to agree to disagree with kindness.

5. Please keep the discussion focused on your own thoughts, feelings, questions, and observations.

6. Please do not interrupt others. Include everyone in your conversations.

7. If necessary, practice conflict resolution by following Matthew 18:15-17.

8. Attend all sessions. Notify the group facilitator in advance if you cannot attend a session.

9. Arrange the room so that there is a circle of chairs.

10. Refreshments are optional.

11. Begin and end each session with prayer requests and prayer.

Session Agenda
Opening prayer
Welcome and introductions
Icebreaker questions
Review of chapter synopsis
Key discussion questions
Sharing words of encouragement
Scripture study and discussion
Review of practical applications and take-a-ways
Closing summary of the group study, including joys and concerns
Review of tools and resources
Closing prayer

For the Pastor/Facilitator:
The pastor will want to recruit and train leaders/facilitators and begin this small group ministry at a time that is appropriate following a community disaster. This could be as early as one year or as late as three years post disaster. Small groups build social ties that are essential for emotional and spiritual healing.

This group may take many forms. The group can be as small as four participants and a leader. Your first group could be a training group for participants who could then become potential co-facilitators or facilitators. The group size should be no larger than twelve to fifteen. Be sure to close the group membership so that new participants do not disrupt the group's confidentiality and process each week. Starting a new group(s) or making a waiting list are better options. Leadership is always the key!

The leader is encouraged to use humorous stories at the beginning of each session. Humor has health benefits! It reduces stress, lowers blood pressure, and increases overall well-being. This biblical-based program is designed for the group members to also help each other.

The church can order your books in advance or have each person order online. Encourage the participants to purchase a book and read the appropriate chapter of this book prior to each session. Ask them to take notes on observations and questions. Be aware of my commonalities of trauma and grief. However, honor the different experiences and perspectives of each. Notice also how the group dynamics will deepen and broaden the members' worldview, values, and spiritual perspectives.

The recovery group facilitator is to be a spiritual and caring leader who is highly motivated to help others grow in their personal faith. The leader does not need to be an expert in trauma healing or financial knowledge. Teaching the content of the first six chapters will provide the essential basics needed to help individuals grow through their disaster recovery.

COMMUNITY PROMOTION

This small group ministry can provide impact to your church and community in many significant ways. The pastor/group facilitator will want to make an announcement in public worship at least two to three weeks in advance of the first session. Follow-up is suggested with direct mail or e-mail to your members. Promotion through social media will be necessary to reach the community. You may also want to offer an information meeting at least two to three weeks in advance where people can purchase their books and ask questions. Or you may also want to have an information table following worship so people can sign up and purchase their book. Advanced registration is recommended.

Be prepared to start additional groups if necessary. Keep the group size at twelve to fifteen by having a waiting list, if necessary. New groups can start year round based on the need. The best promotion is word of mouth. This new Recovery Group Ministry can change lives and transform your community.

The purpose of your church's Recovery Group Ministry should be clear and concise. Publish your purpose statement. Create your own clear, concise, and compelling statement. For example:

Our Purpose:
To help one another grow to be healthy, spiritual, hope-filled, financially savvy, and compassionate people as we continue to grow and recover from disaster.

VOLUNTEER TRAINING RESOURCES

United Methodist Committee on Relief (UMCOR) and National Volunteer Organizations Active in Disaster provides volunteers with a training booklet, *Ministry of Care*.

This thirty-two page training booklet is available when you attend a training program hosted by your United Methodist Conference disaster coordinator and offers strategies to support the inner emotional and spiritual turmoil that disaster survivors experience. It is highly recommended that volunteers attend the approved training programs of this and other denominational, ecumenical, and church agencies.

A Mission Journey, A Handbook for Volunteers, General Board of Global Ministries of the United Methodist Church (Nashville: Upper Room, 2013).

Willard W. C. Ashley Sr. and Stephen Roberts, *Disaster Spiritual Care: Practical Clergy Responses to Community, Regional, and National Tragedy,* 2nd ed. (Nashville: SkyLight Paths, 2017).

NEXT STEPS
TO VOLUNTEER

1. **UMC Training**. If you have not received training to be a volunteer in disaster response, consider signing up for spiritual and emotional care training (https://www.umcor.org/). Training is offered in your United Methodist conference. Different organizations, denominations, agencies, and churches may also provide disaster response training in your area. Find the training program that best fits your needs, location, and abilities. For example, you may want the UMC Early Response Team training, focused on providing a caring Christian presence in the aftermath of disaster.

2. **Emergency supplies**. Volunteers are also needed to serve in relief supply depots. Many conferences have emergency depot locations in your area. UMCOR has depots located in Baldwin, Louisiana (volunteers@sager brown.org) and Salt Lake City, Utah (westdepot@umcor.org).

3. **Think local.** What are the volunteer opportunity and training needs in your location? Find out and volunteer now through your local church or conference office.

SAMPLE VOLUNTEER COVENANT

As a member of this team I agree to:

Remember that I am representing The United Methodist Church of the Resurrection and, more importantly, Jesus Christ. I will seek to model Jesus in my behavior and attitude.

Be in prayer for my teammates, my team leaders, and those with whom we will be in contact.

Remember that I am a guest visiting at the invitation of my hosts. I will respect their culture without judgment.

Remember that I have come to learn as well as to share. I will resist the temptation to inform our hosts about "how we do things." I'll be open to learning about other people's methods and ideas.

Respect others' view of Christianity in the context of their culture. I recognize that Christianity has many faces around the world, and that the purpose of this trip is to share the love of God and to experience faith lived out in a new setting.

Dress modestly, and only bring luggage and possessions that are determined by Resurrection Mission Ministries to be appropriate for the service needs of the mission and the country's culture.

Develop and maintain a servant's attitude toward all nationals and my teammates. I will demonstrate that I am there to serve others and share Christ, while learning and developing relationships.

Respect the thoughts and ideas of my hosts and team members. I will not dominate conversations or interrupt others when they speak, and I will be patient and respectful of differing opinions.

Respect my team leader(s) and respond positively to his or her decisions. If conflict arises, I will refer to the team guidelines for handling conflict.

Refrain from criticism and gossip about our host(s) and my teammates.

Refrain from complaining, as I recognize that travel can present unexpected and undesirable circumstances; instead of complaining, I will be flexible, constructive, and supportive.

Remember not to be exclusive in my relationships and make every effort to interact with all team members.

Refrain from any activity that could be construed as a special or romantic interest in a national or teammate.

Abstain from the use, purchase, and possession of alcoholic beverages, tobacco,* and illegal drugs from the beginning of the trip to the end, including at the departure airports and en route.

Watch my language, refrain from discussing politics or other sensitive subjects, and avoid references to the military and to other religious groups or practices.

Refrain from teaching or practicing any belief that is not supported by The United Methodist Church.

Attend the mandatory Serve Trip Preparation and Abuse Prevention Training, as well as follow-up meetings.

Participate actively in meetings as well as in mission, through sharing opinions, assisting in finding alternatives when necessary, assuming responsibilities, and honoring decisions.

Keep confidential discussions and personal information shared among team members.

Remember that I can be sent home if there is an irresolvable conflict or lack of adherence to this covenant.

*On trips within the United States, an exception will be made for smokers who agree to abide by our Smoking Guidelines for Domestic Serve Trips.

Print Name: ⎯⎯⎯⎯⎯⎯⎯⎯⎯⎯⎯⎯⎯⎯⎯⎯⎯⎯⎯

⎯⎯⎯⎯⎯⎯⎯⎯⎯⎯⎯⎯⎯⎯⎯⎯⎯⎯⎯⎯⎯⎯⎯⎯⎯⎯

Signature: ⎯⎯⎯⎯⎯⎯⎯⎯⎯⎯⎯⎯⎯⎯⎯⎯⎯⎯⎯⎯⎯

⎯⎯⎯⎯⎯⎯⎯⎯⎯⎯⎯⎯⎯⎯⎯⎯⎯⎯⎯⎯⎯⎯⎯⎯⎯⎯

Country: ⎯⎯⎯⎯⎯⎯⎯⎯⎯⎯⎯⎯⎯⎯⎯⎯⎯⎯⎯⎯⎯⎯

⎯⎯⎯⎯⎯⎯⎯⎯⎯⎯⎯⎯⎯⎯⎯⎯⎯⎯⎯⎯⎯⎯⎯⎯⎯⎯

CLOSING HEALING CEREMONY AND CELEBRATION FOR SMALL GROUP MEMBERS[1]

Welcome

Introduction of the Service

Opening Prayer

Act of Praise (Psalm 103:1-18)

Silent Time of Refection on This Psalm

Receive Prayer Requests from Others

(After each request is made, respond in one voice: Lord, hear our prayers.)

Prayer of Compassion

Holy Scripture Reading (Mark 10:46-52 or Matthew 20:29-34)

Reflection and Response to God's Word (offered by group facilitator)

Silent Prayers of Confession

Assurance of Pardon

Passing the Peace

(Let us offer signs of peace to one another by saying, "The peace of Christ be with you.")

Sharing Holy Communion

Words of Institution for the Lord's Supper (serve Holy Communion)

The Lord's Prayer

Closing Prayer of Gratitude

Invitation to Anointing with Oil and Healing Service of the Body, Mind, and Soul

Silent Prayer for One Another

Sharing Our Thanksgivings and Joys

Dismissal (with Romans 15:13 as the Blessing)

Invite members to share a fellowship meal following service

NOTES

Introduction: The Path to Healing

1. Dave Petley, "The Ten Most Important 'Natural' Disasters of the Last Ten Years," *The Landslide Blog*, American Geophysical Union, January 7, 2010, https://blogs.agu.org/landslideblog/2010/01/07/the-ten-most-important-natural -disasters-of-the-last-ten-years/.

Chapter 1: Relief—How the Church Can Help

1. Attributed to mixed martial arts master and champion lightweight boxer Frankie Perez (b. 1989). It is a modern variant of the ancient quote of the Greek Stoic philosopher Epictetus.

2. Eleanor Roosevelt, *You Learn by Living: Seven Keys for a More Fulfilling Life*, anniversary ed. (New York: Harper, 2011), 12.

3. Bob Deits, *Life after Loss: A Practical Guide to Renewing Your Life after Experiencing Major Loss* (New York: Da Capo, 2017), 2.

4. Shelby Lorman, "Why Some Communities Recover Better after Natural Disasters," *Thrive Global*, November 17, 2017, https://thriveglobal.com/stories/why -some-communities-recover-better-after-natural-disasters/.

5. American Red Cross national poll, October 5–8, 2001, by Caravan ORC, International (Poll of 1,000 adults over the age of 18 living in private homes; +/-3%; release date: October 16, 2001; in Willard W. C. Ashley Sr., Stephen B. Roberts, eds., *Disaster Spiritual Care: Practical Clergy Responses to Community, Regional and National Tragedy*, 2nd ed. (Nashville: SkyLight Paths, 2017), xiii.

6. Commentary from Kenneth Carder's interview with Jane Cage. For more information, see Joplin Pays It Forward, www.joplinmo.org/joplin, and www.jane cage.com.

7. John Trent and Gary Smalley, *The Blessing: Giving the Gift of Unconditional Love and Acceptance*, rev. updated ed. (Nashville: Thomas Nelson, 2011).

8. For further information, see "Recovering Emotionally from Disaster," American Psychological Association, www.apa.org/helpcenter/recovering-disasters .aspx.

9. Daniel Aldrich, *Building Resilience: Social Capital in Post-Disaster Recovery* (Chicago: University of Chicago Press, 2012).

10. John A Robinson Jr. quoted in Kathryn M. Haueisen and Carol H. Flores, *A Ready Hope: Effective Disaster Ministry for Congregations*, (Herndon, VA: Alban Institute, 2009), 148.

11. For more information, see "Texas Recovers," Texas Annual Conference, United Methodist Church, www.txcumc.org/txrecovers).

Chapter 2: Recovery—Five Steps for Trauma Healing

1. Harold S. Kushner, *When Bad Things Happen to Good People* (New York: Anchor Books, 1981).

2. Harold S. Kushner, *Nine Essential Things I've Learned About Life,* reprint ed. (New York: Anchor Books, 2016).

3. Peter Levin with Ann Frederick, *Waking the Tiger: Healing Trauma* (Berkeley, CA: North Atlantic Books, 1997), 2.

4. Levin, *Waking the Tiger,* 12.

5. Mari L. McCarthy, *Journaling Power: How to Create the Happy, Healthy Life You Want to Live* (self-pub., Hasmark, 2016).

6. Max Lucado, *Anxious for Nothing: Finding Calm in a Chaotic World* (Nashville: Thomas Nelson, 2017).

7. Howard Clinebell Jr., *Growth Groups* (Nashville: Abingdon Press, 1977).

8. David K. Switzer. *The Dynamics of Grief: Its Source, Pain, and Healing* (Nashville: Abingdon Press, 1970).

Chapter 3: Restoration—Reigniting Hope

1. Anne Lamott, *Bird by Bird: Some Instructions on Writing and Life* (New York: Anchor, 1994), xxiii.

2. Jane Cage, ed., *Joplin Pays It Forward: Community Leaders Share Our Recovery Lessons* (self pub., Amazon, 2013). For further information, see www.joplinmo.org/joplinpaysitforward.

3. Adam Hamilton, *Unafraid: Living with Courage and Hope in Uncertain Times,* (New York: Convergent, 2018).

4. Bob Deits, *Life after Loss: A Practical Guide to Renewing Your Life after Experiencing Major Loss* (self-pub., Da Capo, 2009), 105.

5. Deits, *Life after Loss,* 110.

6. Deits, *Life after Loss,* 149.

7. C. S. Lewis, *The Problem of Pain,* reprint. (New York: HarperOne, 2015), 91.

8. Pierre Teilhard de Chardin, *The Phenomenon of Man,* trans. Bernard Wall (New York: Harper Perennial, 1955), 265.

9. Harold S. Kushner, foreword to *Man's Search for Meaning,* by Viktor E. Frankl, trans. Ilse Lasch (Boston: Beacon, 2006), x.

10. Etty Hillesum, *An Interrupted Life: The Diaries, 1941–1943 and Letters from Westerbork,* trans. Arnold J. Pomerans (New York: Henry Holt, 1996), 30–31. See also Richard Rohr, "Searching for Meaning," Center for Action and Contemplation, October 15, 2018, https://cac.org/searching-for-meaning-2018-10-15/.

11. Howard Thurman, *Meditations of the Heart*, 2nd ed. (Boston: Beacon, 1981), 8.

12. Richard Rohr, "Gazing Upon the Mystery," Center for Action and Contemplation, October 21, 2018, https://cac.org/gazing-upon-the-mystery-2018-10-21/.

13. Bruce L. Blumer, *Simply Grace: Everyday Glimpses of God* (Nashville: The Upper Room, 2019), 117.

14. Howard Clinebell Jr., *Well Being: A Personal Plan for Exploring and Enriching the Seven Dimensions of Life—Mind, Body, Spirit, Love, Work, Play, the Earth* (Quezon City, Philippines: Kadena Books, 1992), 223.

Part II: Financial Foundations and Recovery

1. From the June 2008 Harvard University commencement speech of J. K. Rowling, "The Fringe Benefits of Failure, and the Importance of Imagination," *The Harvard Gazette*, June 2008. View full text of the speech at https://news.harvard.edu/gazette/story/2008/06/text-of-j-k-rowling-speech/.

Chapter 4: Assessment—Taking Your Financial Pulse

1. Jack Canfield with Mark Victor Hansen and Les Hewitt, *The Power of Focus: How to Hit Your Business, Personal, and Financial Targets with Absolute Certainty* (New York: Random House, 2001), 123.

Chapter 5: Spending Plan—Money Management Strategies

1. From the US Presidential Inaugural Address of Jimmy Carter, quoting his high school teacher, Julia Coleman, January 20, 1977. To read the full speech text, see https://jimmycarterlibrary.gov/assets/documents/speeches/inaugadd.phtm.

2. Dictionary.com.

3. Jessica Dickler, "Credit Card Debt Hits a Record High. It's Time to Make a Payoff Plan," CNBC, January 23, 2018, https://www.cnbc.com/2018/01/23/credit-card-debt-hits-record-high.html.

Chapter 6: Planning—Your Financial Recovery Plan

1. For more information, see the Consumer Finance Protection Bureau, www.consumerfinance.gov/consumer-tools/disasters-and-emergencies/.

2. Jon Daugharthy, Attorney at Law, Overland Park, Kansas, personal interview March 10, 2019.

Chapter 9: Reigniting Hope through Love

1. Reprinted in part with permission from Bruce Blumer, "Why Do You Help?" *Parsonage Parables* (blog), December 8, 2017, https://bruceblumer.com/why-do-you-help/. See also, Bruce Blumer, *Simply Grace: Everyday Glimpses of God* (Nashville: Higher Education and Ministry, The United Methodist Church, 2019).

Appendix G: Closing Healing Ceremony and Celebration for Small Group Members

1. Adapted from James K. Wagner, *Just in Time! Healing Services* (Nashville: Abingdon Press, 2007). We suggest this format for a closing celebration service after completing the small group series. You have likely come a long way. This service will hopefully allow time for celebrating your growth and thanking God for his grace and mercy. We suggest the service be forty-five to sixty minutes long. A fellowship meal could be offered before or after the service.

CPSIA information can be obtained
at www.ICGtesting.com
Printed in the USA
LVHW011049230819
628644LV00002B/2

9 781501 890918